Moments
of Light

Lana Vose

Published by Hemingway Publishers

Cover design by Hemingway Publishers

ISBN: Printed in the United States

www.momentsoflight.com

This page is intentionally blank

Foreword

There are few things more powerful than pausing—to listen inward, to write gently, and to make room for your own presence. In a world that often measures us by movement and output, this journal offers something quieter: an invitation to step out of the rush and arrive fully in yourself. This journal does not aim to fix you, improve you, or reshape you. It simply invites you to meet yourself as you are, in the small and honest moments that often pass unnoticed. To the truths that don't shout, but whisper.

Every page is a quiet invitation. To reflect. To feel. To remember what matters. It doesn't require perfect words or polished thoughts. All it asks is that you come as you are—unfiltered and unhurried.

In these pages, you'll find soft questions, gentle prompts, and space to explore your own rhythms. There is no right way to do this. No rules. Write when you feel ready. Pause when you need. Return when you can. This journal honors your timing, not someone else's structure.

It is easy to lose touch with ourselves in a world that moves so fast. We offer our time to so many things—yet so rarely to our own thoughts. This journal encourages you to claim just a little space each day. To sit. To breathe. To ask yourself, quietly and honestly: *"How am I, really?"*

Over time, these small reflections will echo. Your words become a map back to your center. You may find comfort in your own voice, clarity in your patterns, and tenderness in your unfolding. You may notice how you grow, what you value, and what makes your heart steady.

And when you fill the final page, may you not feel that something is ending—but that something is beginning. A soft threshold into deeper presence. You are building a practice of meeting yourself with care, and there is no finish line to that kind of becoming...

Let this be your gentle companion. Let this be your mirror and your pause. Let this be a soft place to land.

—With warmth, and deep respect for your journey inward.

Introduction

This journal is more than a place to write—it is a refuge, a companion, a mirror. A quiet witness to your unfolding. A place where you are invited not to perform, but to arrive. To slow your pace and meet your inner life not with answers, but with awareness. It is a space that waits for you, no matter how long you've been away.

You may notice that these pages are not divided into neat chapters, nor do they follow a predictable path. That is intentional. Life itself offers no such structure. We make plans and draw timelines, but life unfolds in its own rhythm—sudden joys, deep losses, uncertain middles—all without warning, without script. There is no "right time" to tend to the soul, just as there is no perfect order to the inner work we are called to do. You enter when you're ready, and sometimes even when you're not.

We are always living inside overlapping needs: the need to protect our peace, the need to connect meaningfully with others, and the need to grow, to stretch, to become. None of these can wait for their turn. None should be sacrificed for the comfort of others. Losing our inner peace in the name of connection leaves us depleted. Ignoring our need to grow while tending only to our relationships can make us feel unseen by ourselves. This journal invites you to hold all of it—the full complexity of your emotional landscape—with presence and care. With patience, not pressure. This is the essence of resilience: not perfection, not control, but an ability to stay rooted while the winds of life shift.

Each reflection here weaves between these threads—Inner Peace, Communication, and Growth—not as separate chapters, but as a tapestry. There's no beginning or end—only entrances, moments, invitations. You'll find no linear path, because your healing, your becoming, is not linear. You may return to a page years from now and read it differently, because you have become different. That, too, is the gift of this practice.

Use this space as a daily ritual or an occasional resting place. Choose a time when you can come as you are—unfiltered, unhurried. Let the pen move as it wants. If your thoughts arrive slowly, that is fine. If your feelings are hard to name, be with them anyway. This journal does not ask for eloquence. It asks for honesty. It offers not judgment, but sanctuary.

You might read your words aloud to yourself. You may find your breath deepen as you write. You may surprise yourself with the honesty you've kept tucked away. Let all of it in. Let discomfort be an invitation to curiosity rather than shame. Let insight arrive on its own time—not rushed, not forced.

When you come to the end of these pages, it will not be an ending. If anything, it is a beginning—a tender commitment to listen inward, again and again. Keep this journal. Let it be evidence of your presence in your own life. And when a few years have passed, begin another. Revisit the same questions. Compare the pages, not just for what you've done, but for who you've become.

This is not a book of answers. It is a practice of returning. A gathering of moments that ask you to notice, to feel, to stay.

Let this journal be your conversation with yourself. Your sanctuary. Your remembering.

And may you treat these pages with the same compassion you long to offer to the world—with trust, with tenderness, and with the quiet joy of being fully seen.

The step not taken haunts the dreaming soul,

a silent weight that dulls the living whole.

We fear the dawn for all we do not know—

yet night must end, if light is still our goal.

What if, beyond the fear, a garden lay?

What if, through change, we find a brighter way?

The cage feels safe until we lift our eyes—

and see the skies we've longed for, day by day.

Unhappy hearts are calls we must not shun,

a whisper that our inner work's begun.

To stay unchanged is sorrow, slow and deep—

but change, though steep, can lead us to the sun.

A single step—though trembling, full of doubt—

can turn the soul's dim silence inside out.

Begin, and let the old world fade behind—

the life you seek is waiting to be found

Weekly Practice

Set aside ten minutes each day to sit in quiet. Let there be no music, no conversation, no screens—only the tender rhythm of your breath and the flicker of passing thoughts. Choose a place where silence can find you: near a window bathed in early light, curled on the floor, nestled beneath branches in a quiet garden. Let the environment be simple and kind. Wherever the silence can meet you. If thoughts arise, notice them like clouds drifting across a wide sky. There is nothing to fix, nothing to change. You are not here to edit yourself—you are here to listen. Feel the gentle weight of your form grounded in stillness. This is your pause from doing. A moment where you are not measured by output, by words, or by urgency. Let your body soften and settle as you rest in this pause from doing. You are not wasting time—you are steeping in presence. This stillness is not empty; it is full of unseen restoration. Feel how your breath anchors you—not just to this moment, but to yourself. With practice, this quiet will no longer feel like an absence. It will begin to feel like an arrival. Like turning gently toward a part of you that's been waiting.

This is not an escape—but like a gentle homecoming.

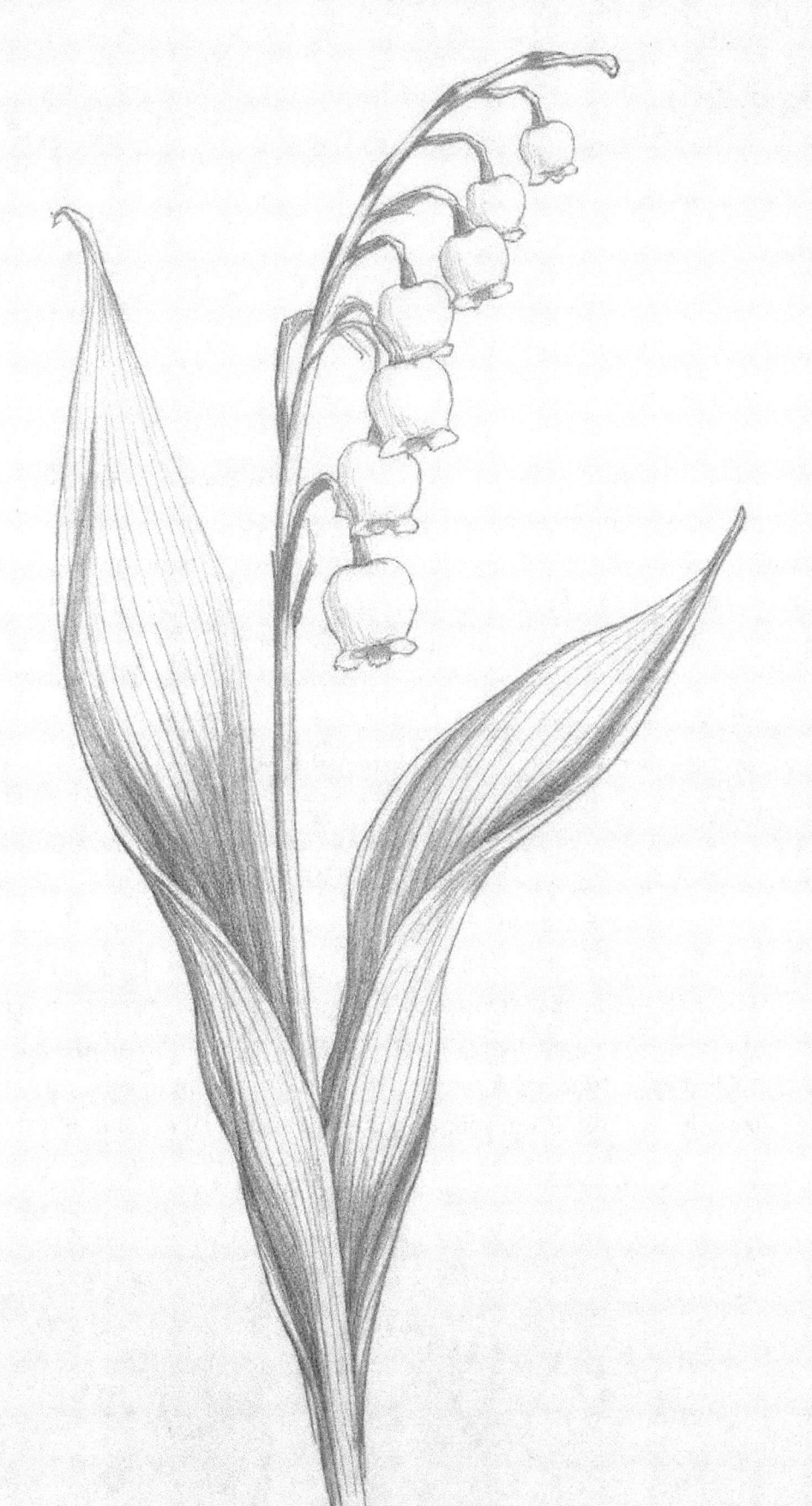

DAY 1

Mug warm in your hand,

the sun not yet demanding—

soul remembers home.

Before your name is spoken, your inbox checked, your mask of readiness worn—pause. Step into a pocket of time that belongs only to you. This space, before the world begins to tug at your sleeves, is not for productivity but for remembrance. Let your body decide the ritual: a warm mug pressed to your chest, bare feet settling into the cool floor, or eyes drifting toward the slow yawn of morning light. Let your gestures be tender and slow. Instead of moving outward, practice the gentle art of arriving inward. Breathe not out of habit, but as if your safety depends on it—not shallow and quick, but from the base of your spine, allowing each inhale to gather your scattered parts gently, patiently. You don't need to rush this gathering. Ask without urgency: What would it feel like to belong completely to myself, right here? You might not know the answer—and that's okay. Asking is itself a quiet act of courage. Write one sentence in your journal—skip the to-do lists. Speak instead to who you wish to be as you move through this day. If pain rises, welcome it as a messenger. If calm appears, let it linger, not clutched too tightly but held in open hands. Stillness is not the absence of movement, but a presence of truth —an anchoring beneath all the rushing. Let this daily ritual become a threshold—not a doorway from rest into chaos, but from forgetfulness to gentle remembering. A passage into your own presence before the world calls you away.

What ritual—however simple—helps you feel rooted at the edges of your day Write about one way it nourishes you. ?

_____

_____

_____

_____

_____

_____

_____

_____

_____

_____

_____

_____

_____

_____

_____

_____

_____

_____

_____

_____

_____

_____

_____

DAY 2

Steps trace silent paths,

breath stretches beyond the rush—

Stillness speaks in waves.

The world around you moves with relentless momentum, but your breath and steps can resist the tide, quietly and without resistance. Slow your gait intentionally—feel the weight of your feet meeting the earth, the subtle textures beneath them, and the rhythm that your body naturally seeks when unhurried. Allow the space between tasks to grow spacious. Expand it by extending your exhale longer than your inhale, offering your nervous system a softened place to land. Listen, too, for the silences that shape your speech when you take part in a conversation. Hold those pauses gently rather than rushing to fill them. Let stillness speak. Ask yourself, not as a passing thought but as a pulse beneath your skin: What am I pursuing, and does it demand my urgency now? Sense where tension accumulates in your body as this question settles—does your heart quicken, or does it ease? Let that awareness guide you—helping you discern what deserves your full attention, and what can be allowed to dissolve into quiet. Design moments of deliberate rhythm—a slow breath before opening your email, a mindful swallow of water between meetings, or a moment of skyward gaze before making a decision—each act, subtle as it may be, becomes a reclamation of your own tempo. This is a defiance against the noise of acceleration, a reclamation of your innate pace as an act of self-respect. Allow life's rapid currents to flow. Stand steady in your own. Your cadence doesn't need to keep pace with noise—it is a quiet current shaped by intention, deep and unshakeable.

Which moments today whispered the clearest truth about your own rhythm and presence?

_____

_____

_____

_____

_____

_____

_____

_____

_____

_____

_____

_____

_____

_____

_____

_____

_____

_____

_____

_____

_____

_____

_____

DAY 3

She asked too often,

until I forgot how to breathe—

the gate swings no more.

Sometimes, it is not your own carelessness, but another's weight that bends the fence. You notice their questions come too quickly, their presence feels too constant, and their needs are spoken louder than yours. A friend, a partner, a colleague—someone you care for—reaches past what you're willing to give, not out of cruelty, but out of habit. And in your silence, that habit grows like ivy, curling further each day around what you've never voiced. Boundaries with others are hardest when love is involved. We fear seeming cold, distant, or disloyal. We worry that asserting limits will fracture what we've worked so tenderly to hold together. But how much of yourself you allow to be consumed is not a measure of love—it is a measure of erosion. Compassion is not boundless if it leaves you empty. Begin by identifying the moment you felt overrun. Was it a conversation that left you breathless with exhaustion? A favor that felt like an obligation? A request that ignored your own limits? Sit with that moment and ask yourself—not to judge, but to understand—*what have I allowed, and what am I no longer able to sustain?* This awareness is not selfish. It's sacred. Instead of retreating or tolerating, explore how to express your threshold clearly. Not to punish others, but to protect the relationship from resentment. Let your words be simple, steady, and clear: "When you ask this of me, I feel stretched thin," or "I want to be there for you, but I need space too." Speak plainly, not apologetically. Speak not to blame, but to reveal your truth before it turns bitter. Sometimes the kindest act is to show someone where the line is—so neither of you continues pretending it doesn't exist. By holding the boundary, you give the relationship the chance to breathe honestly. You teach them how to love you better.

Think of someone you care for deeply. What boundary have you placed with them, and how can you feel grateful for the strength it took—and the honesty it may invite into your connection?

_____

_____

_____

_____

_____

_____

_____

_____

_____

_____

_____

_____

_____

_____

_____

_____

_____

_____

_____

_____

_____

_____

_____

_____

DAY 4

I whispered, "not now" —

and the world kept turning on.

I was not undone.

There is a strength in refusal that speaks without noise—one that asks you to stand still while the world urges you to bend. Saying no can feel like betrayal, especially if you've spent years cushioning others from disappointment and becoming fluent in the language of overextension. But each time you agree when your spirit says otherwise, you build a life that belongs to someone else. A life co-authored by expectation and the avoidance of discomfort. Guilt thrives in the space between your truth and your performance—it grows in the silence left by the words you couldn't bear to say. When you say yes, ask: Who am I protecting? And what part of myself am I abandoning? Notice the reflex—the instant nod, the smile that doesn't reach your eyes, the rehearsed justification tumbling from your mouth. Let that be your first shift: not toward guilt, but toward awareness. You don't need an elaborate excuse to protect your peace. You are allowed to disappoint others to remain true to yourself. Practice a simple phrase you can carry like armor: "That doesn't work for me right now." Say it aloud. Hear the shape of your boundary take form in your own voice. Let the discomfort rise—but do not rush to smooth it over. Guilt will visit, but it is not a sign you've done wrong; it's only a sign that you are rewriting the rules. You are stepping out of a script you didn't consent to. Every no you speak with clarity makes room for a deeper yes— to rest, to alignment, to the life you're meant to live rather than someone else's version to live. Protecting your peace is not selfish. It's the soil from which all true generosity grows. It's where love, given freely and not out of obligation, finally has a chance to flourish.

Recall a time you said no and honored what you needed instead. What shifted in you or around you as a result—and how can you thank yourself for choosing peace over pleasing?

_____

_____

_____

_____

_____

_____

_____

_____

_____

_____

_____

_____

_____

_____

_____

_____

_____

_____

_____

_____

_____

_____

_____

DAY 5

I spoke what I need—

not louder, just without shame.

And still, I belonged.

The need to explain is often born from a deeper fear: Will they still accept me if I do what I need? You string together reasons like a shield—just enough evidence to earn the right to care for yourself. But your needs are not courtroom arguments. They do not require permission slips or performance. Every time you elaborate beyond what's true for you, a little piece of your inner authority is surrendered. You begin to trade authenticity for approval, honesty for harmony. Pay close attention to the moments you start to over-explain—when your voice rushes, when your fingers type too much, when your eyes are padded with discomfort rather than clarity. What are you trying to prove, and to whom? Begin a practice of brevity—not as dismissal, but as self-trust. Choose one current need—rest, space, time, support—and state it in a sentence, no more. Let it be clean, unadorned, whole. Try: "I won't be joining tonight," or "I'm not available this weekend." Say it aloud. Notice what rises in your body—a tightening, a second-guessing, a flutter of guilt, the instinct to soften your message or add a footnote of reassurance. Stay with it. That discomfort is not a sign you are wrong; it is the stretch of reclaiming your voice. You are not selfish for wanting to protect your time. You are not rude in prioritizing your capacity. You are not unkind for asking less of yourself when the world demands more. Your needs are genuine, and they do not have to be explained to be honored. You do not owe anyone your exhaustion as proof of your love.

This is your declaration: not of rebellion, but of return. A homecoming to yourself, spoken one unadorned truth at a time.

Think of a time when you stated what you needed without defending it. What did you protect yourself by doing so—and how can you thank yourself for trusting your truth without apology?

_____

_____

_____

_____

_____

_____

_____

_____

_____

_____

_____

_____

_____

_____

_____

_____

_____

_____

_____

_____

_____

_____

_____

DAY 6

Once I feared the fire—

now I see how ash and flame

cleared the path I walk.

Certain experiences stay with us, not only because they hurt, but because they changed us. They leave imprints on our memory and shape our sense of self. Think of a challenge you once met with dread or trembling. Maybe it was a difficult conversation, a profound loss, a painful leaving, or the quiet ache of letting go. At the time, it may have felt like too much, too sharp, too soon. And yet, you moved through it. Not untouched, but undeniably changed. What part of you did that challenge awaken or fortify? Did it teach you to speak when silence felt safer? To choose yourself when approval was tempting? To hold grief without letting it consume your identity? These jagged moments often call forth a strength we didn't know we had. They stretch us in ways that are rarely graceful but always profound. Write it down. Name the ways you stretched, even if the growth was not graceful. Return to who you were before that challenge. What beliefs did you carry that no longer hold true? Perhaps you thought strength meant never breaking, or that love required self-abandonment. Maybe you believed peace was something to be earned, rather than something to be claimed. Trace the difference between then and now—not as a linear improvement, but as a widening. You didn't just become stronger; you became more spacious. More capable of holding contradiction, sitting with uncertainty, and honoring complexity. Your resilience may not have arrived with fanfare, but it is present in how you now face difficulty, protect your peace, and recognize what you once couldn't name. This is not about romanticizing pain. It is about reclaiming authorship over your becoming. You did not just survive—you remade yourself with the pieces. You are not defined by what broke you, but by how you chose to rebuild. So honor the quiet victories. You are a mosaic of every choice, every scar, every stretch you made for yourself. And that, in itself, is a masterpiece.

What inner strength or clarity did this challenge uncover in you—and how can you thank yourself for facing what once frightened you, not by force, but through persistence, courage, and care for who you were becoming?

_____

_____

_____

_____

_____

_____

_____

_____

_____

_____

_____

_____

_____

_____

_____

_____

_____

_____

_____

_____

DAY 7

Edges pulled me down,

but something unnamed held on—

a thread stitched in hope.

It can feel as if the threads are slipping when your burdens meet the raw edge of what you have left to give. Perhaps exhaustion twisted around your spirit, or the emptiness that follows unmet needs. You reached a point when giving up did not just seem reasonable—it felt like the only remaining option. And yet, you did not. What stopped you? Was it love for someone who needed you? A promise you made to yourself or someone else not to break? A whisper of hope, too small to explain but too real to ignore? Trace it now. Write it down. Name the reasons that tethered you to yourself when it would have been easier to let go. Perhaps the reason was insignificant; you had not recounted your experiences, or you still believed in a modicum of recovery. What part of you decided to stay? What were you protecting, even when everything hurts? You may have felt fractured, but even broken things have instincts for preservation. Honor that version of you—not for being fearless, but for being deeply human and holding on through uncertainty. For choosing breath over silence, movement over surrender, hope over finality. Now, reflect on who you have become because of that choice. What have you learned about your capacity to endure? What tenderness did you uncover in the aftermath of staying? What boundaries did you begin to build once you saw you deserved more than collapse? Maybe you started saying no. Maybe you stopped apologizing for needing rest. Maybe you began to see your worth not as something to earn, but as something inherent. Let this memory become a reminder: your strength was never loud—it was in the decision to keep breathing, keep walking, keep hoping when you did not know what the next step would offer.

What part of you refused to let go when everything felt like too much—and how can you thank that inner thread of resilience for carrying you forward into the life you are still writing now?

_____

_____

_____

_____

_____

_____

_____

_____

_____

_____

_____

_____

_____

_____

_____

_____

_____

_____

_____

_____

_____

_____

_____

Weekly Practice

Choose one person whose presence you value and reach out to them with sincerity. Let this be a moment that asks nothing but offers everything. This could be a phone call where your voice holds warmth, a walk shared in soft conversation, or a message that says something real and unguarded. Let your words reveal something tender—perhaps gratitude for the way they've stood by you, an apology long held in silence, a memory that still grows, or a simple care that asks nothing in return. Do not seek performance; seek truth. Ask how they are really doing and wait to listen. Share without rehearsing. Be open to silence between you. Notice what shifts when connection is given freely, without needing anything in return. Let this gesture—however small—carry the weight of your heart's intention.

DAY 8

Quiet threads unravel,

stillness blooms beneath the noise—

home in every breath.

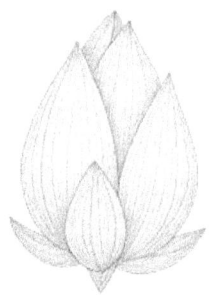

Silence is often mistaken for emptiness—an absence, a void, something to be filled or avoided. Yet it holds the shape of a doorway waiting to open. Invite yourself to sit without distraction—no devices, no background noise, no interruptions—and feel how the stillness inhabits your skin, your breath, the subtle spaces between thoughts. At first, it may feel unfamiliar, even uncomfortable. But discomfort is not a warning—it is a teacher. When discomfort arises, meet it without resistance, allowing it to pass like a visitor whose presence teaches, not threatens. Notice the urge to escape silence—whether through movement, mental chatter, or reaching for sound—and redirect your attention. Instead of following that impulse, pause. Redirect your attention. Stay anchored. Ask yourself: What might surface if I stay anchored here, refusing to fill the space? Observe how the tension around silence loosens as presence deepens, revealing a reservoir of clarity and calm you had not anticipated. Begin by choosing one moment in your day for this practice—perhaps between tasks or before sleep—and extend it as your capacity grows. Track the changes in how silence feels: from disarray to sanctuary, from absence to source. Let this developing relationship recalibrate your experience of noise and busyness, anchoring you in a steadiness that transcends circumstance. Within this safe space, discover the steady pulse of your own being calling you home.

What did your silence reveal today that words could not capture?

DAY 9

Breath beneath the noise,

truth drifts in like morning mist—

unseen, but steady.

Within the restless tides of your mind, subtle currents of feeling pulse, awaiting your recognition. These inner signals often go unnoticed, drowned out by the rush toward action or the noise of daily demands. But beneath the surface, your body speaks in sensations, your emotions whisper in rhythms. To hear them is to begin the journey inward. Pause. Instead of moving quickly toward action, explore where your body's sensations anchor you—does a tightness clutch your chest, or a gentle warmth ease your belly? Invite yourself to name these sensations and emotions with a patient, compassionate gaze, allowing their stories to surface without interruption or correction. What fears, hopes, or truths lie beneath the mental chatter that often demands your attention? This act of naming is not small—it is sacred. It transforms fleeting impressions into a map. Journaling these discoveries transforms fleeting impressions into a map, revealing recurring motifs that illuminate your deepest needs and desires. In writing, you give shape to the formless, voice to the silent. When overwhelm clouds your clarity, returning to this inner dialogue can ground you, restoring connection with your authentic self. Notice how this attentive listening shifts your relationship with challenges—do they soften, expand, or reveal new pathways? This is not about solving every problem. It's about staying present with what is real. It's about choosing sincerity over reaction, depth over speed. Let your inner signals become an unwavering compass, steering you toward choices rooted in sincerity rather than reaction. Through this tender cultivation of presence, you nurture a sanctuary within—where healing, wisdom, and grace unfold between each breath. Where you meet yourself not with critique, but with care

Reflect on one subtle feeling or insight that revealed itself today. What wisdom did it offer you, and how can you honor it as a guide in your journey?

_____

_____

_____

_____

_____

_____

_____

_____

_____

_____

_____

_____

_____

_____

_____

_____

_____

_____

_____

_____

_____

_____

_____

DAY 10

Not every shared space

leaves you nourished when you leave—

some rooms steal your fire.

Energy leaves clues before your mind understands the message. In certain relationships, you may feel a heaviness in your chest after a conversation, or a need to recover after simply being near someone. These aren't coincidences. They are invitations to look closer. Begin by mapping your recent interactions. Reflect on the people you've spent time with, spoken to, or thought about. Which connections leave you feeling hollow, irritable, or unsure of yourself? Which of them sparks overthinking, self-doubt, or emotioVnal fatigue? Pay attention to the physical responses in your body: the tension in your shoulders, the tightness in your jaw, the ache in your stomach. These are not just reactions—they are data. Write down the names, the patterns, and the physical responses in your body. This is not about blame—it is about recognition. Are you shrinking here to stay safe? Are you overcompensating to keep peace? Are you being asked to carry more than I receive? Choose one of these relationships and imagine adjusting the boundary around it. What would shift if you said less, offered less, or delayed your response? What if you allowed the silence to speak instead of rushing to fill the gaps? Test this. Choose a simple change—a shorter reply, a longer pause, a declined invitation—and observe what shifts, both in the dynamic and within you. Does your body feel lighter? Does your mind quiet? Does your spirit begin to reclaim space? Not every connection deserves equal access to your spirit. Your energy is not infinite, and your presence is not a debt. It is an offering, and offerings must be chosen, not drained. The more you track where your light dims, the more you will learn where to stay—and where to step back.

Bring to mind a relationship where you have recently honored your own capacity—either by stepping back or by asking for balance. What gratitude can you offer yourself for listening to your energy rather than overriding it?

_____

_____

_____

_____

_____

_____

_____

_____

_____

_____

_____

_____

_____

_____

_____

_____

_____

_____

_____

_____

_____

_____

_____

DAY 11

The line was crossed once—

still, I can paint it anew

with steadier hands.

When a boundary is violated, the wound is often twofold—the ache of the crossing itself, and the self-doubt that follows. You may replay the moment, wondering if you were too vague, too forgiving, too slow to speak. But boundaries are not ruined by one rupture. They are living agreements—capable of being redrawn, reinforced, reclaimed. Begin with the truth. Start with clarity. What happened that felt like too much, too fast, or too deep? Write it directly, without cushioning the discomfort. Notice if your impulse is to excuse the other's behavior, or to turn inward with blame. Instead, name the impact without dilution. What shifted in you when your limit was not honored? What were you left holding that was not yours? This naming is the first step in repair. It affirms that your experience matters, even if it was dismissed or misunderstood. Repair starts with reaffirming your own worthiness to be respected—even if the other person never sees it. Speak your boundary again, more clearly this time. You do not have to explain the past; you only need to define the present. Say it simply: "That did not feel okay. I need something different from now on." Let your tone be anchored, not harsh. The aim is not punishment, but restoration. If trust was harmed, it may take time to rebuild—or it may require distance. Allow yourself to decide what repair looks like for you, not what makes the other most comfortable. You are not obligated to resume closeness, to forgive quickly, or to pretend nothing happened. You are allowed to choose healing over harmony. Boundaries violated do not make you weak; they reveal where greater clarity is needed. The repair is a form of reclamation—a return to your own inner authority.

When have you had to reestablish a boundary that someone overlooked or overstepped? How did that act of repair reflect your deepening self-respect—and what gratitude can you offer yourself for choosing healing over avoidance?

_____

_____

_____

_____

_____

_____

_____

_____

_____

_____

_____

_____

_____

_____

_____

_____

_____

_____

_____

_____

_____

_____

_____

DAY 12

The ground took me in —

then something stirred in the dark,

reminding me: rise.

When the world has pressed hard against your chest and you have sunk into stillness—not from rest but from defeat—the idea of rising again can feel unreachable. But again and again, you have. Not always quickly. Not always flawless. But something in you has chosen to rise—not just to return to function, but to re-enter life on your own terms. That choice, however quiet, is a testament to your resilience. Recall when you felt knocked down—by loss, by disappointment, by betrayal, by exhaustion. What was it that helped you move again? Was it the rhythm of a routine, the steadiness of a friend's voice, the words of a book, the grounding of your own breath? Write what helped, even if it felt insignificant. These are not just comforts, they are clues. What anchors you when you lose your sense of direction? Consider the patterns of care that bring you back into connection with yourself. Is it solitude, movement, honest conversation, art, faith, or nature? You do not need to wait for collapse to access them. Build a list, a ritual, a gentle structure that honors your return to self when the world frays your edges. What does rising actually mean to you? Is it reclaiming your voice? Is it forgiving yourself? Is it simply deciding that despair will not be your final language? Let your definition be yours alone. Every time you have risen, you have redefined resilience—not as perfection, but as willingness. Rising doesn't mean you were never down. It means you chose to become again. And each time, you will do so with more clarity, more grace, and more truth.

What resources—inner or outer—have helped you rise when you thought you couldn't? How can you offer gratitude to the resilience that lives in you, and to the supports that waited patiently until you were ready to stand again?

_____

_____

_____

_____

_____

_____

_____

_____

_____

_____

_____

_____

_____

_____

_____

_____

_____

_____

_____

_____

_____

_____

DAY 13

The fall split the road,

but underneath the breaking

was a hidden root.

Failure has a sound—sometimes it is the thud of expectations collapsing, other times the silence after no one answers. It can echo in your chest, linger in your thoughts, and shape the way you carry yourself for days. And yet, what we call failure is often just the place where control ends and learning begins. Reframing it asks for courage—not to deny the sting, but to see through it. To ask: What if the place you stumbled was never a detour, but part of the shaping? Think of something you tried that did not unfold the way you hoped. Recall how it felt in your body—in your breath, in your self-talk, in the way you held your shoulders for days afterward. What did you learn—not about the task, but about yourself? Did you discover where you attach your worth? Or realize you needed different support? Maybe it revealed a truth you were trying not to see. Write what the failure asked you to reckon with. Did it push you toward humility, boundaries, or creativity? Did it show you what matters more than being right or being liked? Did it move you closer to something more aligned, even if it arrived by way of undoing? Now, write a sentence that begins with: "Because I failed, I now know..." Let that truth guide your future attempts. Consider what failure protected you from—was it a path that would have demanded self-abandonment? Or an identity that no longer fits? Failure does not mean you were wrong to try. It means you were brave enough to risk something, and human enough to grow from the rupture. You are not defined by what didn't work. You are shaped by what you learned and how you choose to move forward.

What unexpected insight or resilience did failure offer you—and how can you honor the ways it refined you, rather than reduced you, along your journey of becoming?

_____

_____

_____

_____

_____

_____

_____

_____

_____

_____

_____

_____

_____

_____

_____

_____

_____

_____

_____

_____

_____

_____

_____

DAY 14

Once it meant holding—

now strength looks like letting go,

crying without shame.

Once, strength might have been measured by how well you hid the hurt, how tightly you held yourself in place. You might have praised yourself for pushing through, for staying silent, for doing what was expected even when your heart was breaking. That version of strength was forged in survival. It taught you how to endure, how to protect, how to persist. But now—perhaps—strength has begun to take on new shapes. It could look like asking for help before the breaking point. Maybe it is being able to say, "I do not know," or "I need time." Maybe it is choosing rest even when the world rewards exhaustion. This evolution is not a weakness; it is wisdom. It means you have unlearned what kept you armored and relearned how to meet life with more truth. What did you once believe strength required of you? Did it demand perfection? Endurance without complaint? Denial of your needs? What does strength require of you now? Honesty? Surrender? Boundaries? Forgiveness? Let your answers live beside each other; neither is wrong, but one was built for survival, and the other for healing. Trace this transition not as a clean break, but a gradual unfolding. Write about when you acted from your new definition, even if the old one still tugged at you. How did it feel in your body, your relationships, your spirit? The world may not always recognize this kind of strength— but you do. And that is enough to keep walking with it.

What new version of strength have you grown into, and how can you thank yourself for choosing authenticity over appearance, tenderness over toughness, and truth over the need to prove your worth?

_____

_____

_____

_____

_____

_____

_____

_____

_____

_____

_____

_____

_____

_____

_____

_____

_____

_____

_____

_____

_____

_____

Weekly Practice

Choose one day this week to set down your screens and untangle from the constant buzz of input. Turn off notifications. Let emails wait. Step away from the glow of devices. Return to the rhythm of your body, of wind moving through leaves, of a book's quiet patience. Notice how time stretches when you are not rushing to fill it. Cook a meal slowly. Watch the light shift across the walls. Be present with someone without the filter of a screen. Let this day be a retreat, a return to the texture of your life. As the digital world fades, feel what comes alive again inside of you. You may find that creativity stirs, that clarity returns, that joy flickers in unexpected places. You may find that what felt distant—your intuition, your peace, your sense of self—was never gone, only buried beneath the noise.

DAY 15

In the breath before,

silence shapes the path ahead—

truth waits in the pause.

Between stimulus and response, there is a narrow doorway—silent, potent, easily missed. It is here, in this sliver of time, that the path to intentional living begins. When your chest tightens with anger, or anxiety stirs beneath your ribs, bring your focus to the rhythm of your breathing—not to escape, but to witness. Let your breath become an anchor, gently pulling you into presence. Notice where your body clenches or retreats. These physical responses are signals—guardians of something tender within. What are you guarding? What longing is hidden here? Let yourself linger in this space without rushing to resolution, like holding a fragile truth in your palm. You are not the prisoner of your reaction—you are the one who can choose whether to feed it or listen beneath it. In these seconds of pause, invite your deeper self to speak: What would it look like to respond from integrity, rather than impulse? What does honesty look like, felt in the body and translated into action? Practice anchoring your decisions in this breath-length of reflection. It won't always be easy—but over time, this will become your revolution—a way of being in both your inner world and the world around you.

Name a moment today when you paused before reacting. What clarity emerged from that space, and what does it reveal about who you are becoming?

_____

_____

_____

_____

_____

_____

_____

_____

_____

_____

_____

_____

_____

_____

_____

_____

_____

_____

_____

_____

_____

_____

_____

_____

DAY 16

Breath like ocean tides—

anchoring the heart's wild sway,

softening the storm.

Your breath does not rush you—it waits, unwavering, even when the world pulls you in every direction. In moments when emotions surge like waves—grief tightening your throat, anger quickening your pulse—pause. Bring your full attention to how your body holds your breath. Is your inhale stuck in your chest? Is your exhale fleeing before completion? Place one hand on your chest and the other on your lower abdomen. Breathe in slowly through your nose until your lower hand lifts—gently. Then release through your mouth, extending the exhale just slightly longer than the inhale. Stay with this rhythm, not to push feelings away, but to widen the space in which they can be understood. As the breath steadies, ask: What is this feeling truly asking of me—comfort, expression, boundaries, rest? With time, the breath becomes more than survival—it becomes a teacher, returning you to yourself amid intensity. Let it guide you not toward perfection, but toward presence. In this space, shaped by breath and awareness, transformation begins—not as a performance, but as a gentle becoming.

Recall a moment today when your breath helped you stay with a hard emotion. What did it reveal or change within you?

_____

_____

_____

_____

_____

_____

_____

_____

_____

_____

_____

_____

_____

_____

_____

_____

_____

_____

_____

_____

_____

_____

_____

_____

DAY 17

Breath shifts like the tide,

carrying whispers within—

truth beneath the waves.

Across the rhythm of your day, your breath carries messages your mind may not yet perceive. Notice how it changes as you move through unique moments—whether walking softly, engaging in work, listening deeply, or speaking with intention. Is your breath steady and full, or clipped and rushed? Observe how it tightens when pressure mounts or eases in times of calm. Begin to trace these patterns back to the emotions that stir beneath the surface. They're not always loud—but they're always present. To deepen this awareness, consider keeping a simple log for one day: note what you were doing, what emotion was present, and how your breath responded. This is not a practice of judgment, but an invitation to deepen your relationship with yourself. When you become aware of your constricted breath, gently encourage it to widen and lengthen—allowing space for ease to grow. Over time, this embodied awareness becomes a compass, guiding you toward days lived with more grace, clarity, and tenderness. Each breath becomes a conversation with your deeper self, unfolding the intimate map of your inner world—one moment at a time.

Dig into your day to find when paying attention to your breath revealed something new about how you felt. How did this awareness shape your experience of that day?

_____

_____

_____

_____

_____

_____

_____

_____

_____

_____

_____

_____

_____

_____

_____

_____

_____

_____

_____

_____

_____

_____

_____

_____

DAY 18

Their presence settles —

not by silence, but by truth.

I do not perform.

Some people in your life do not require you to shrink and reshape yourself. Around them, your laughter is unmeasured, your pauses unfilled, your needs uncamouflaged. You do not scan their faces for approval, nor rehearse words in your head before they are spoken. This ease is not accidental—it is the outcome of emotional safety, trust, and a mutual honoring of presence. Walk back through the echoes of your recent conversations—what tones still resonate within you? Who leaves you feeling lighter, not because they entertain or distract, but because you did not have to hide? Think of those who made room for all of you: your boundaries, your hesitations, your joy, and your grief without trying to reshape any of them? List their names. Reflect on how your body feels in their company—was your breath smooth or shallow? Did your shoulders drop, your voice soften? What allowed you to exhale? *What is it about them that allows you to exhale? What do they do—or not do—that grants you that kind of ease?* Perhaps they listen without rushing to respond. Perhaps they do not expect performance or perfection. Perhaps they remember what matters to you and hold it with care. This reflection is not just about noticing them—it is about understanding the conditions that support your wholeness. Once you know what makes you feel safe, you can seek it intentionally and offer it in return. You can choose relationships that mirror that ease, rather than drain it. And you can recognize that this kind of comfort is not rare—it is simply aligned. It's what happens when presence meets acceptance. You do not owe all of yourself to every room. But you owe yourself the grace of choosing where you are fully allowed to be.

Call to mind someone around whom you feel unguarded, unrushed, and whole. What is their presence that invites such ease—and how can you express gratitude, in words or in action, for the way they honor the real you?

_____

_____

_____

_____

_____

_____

_____

_____

_____

_____

_____

_____

_____

_____

_____

_____

_____

_____

_____

_____

_____

_____

_____

DAY 19

What if love was this—

a meeting with no demand,

just space to remain?

Beneath all the layers of adaptation—beneath the roles you've learned to play—there lives a longing to be met without distortion. What would it mean to be in a relationship where you are not managing perception, not diluting your needs or reshaping to fit someone else's comfort, where translation isn't required just to be understood. Begin here: What does it feel like to be truly at ease with another person? Not the surface calm of politeness, but the deep steadiness of being accepted as you are, with no need to shrink or stretch. Imagine an ideal relationship—not perfect, not without struggle, but deeply reciprocal. What qualities would it hold? What would safety feel like in this bond? Would there be room to say no without consequence? Would your needs be acknowledged with curiosity instead of resistance? Would love be measured by presence, not performance? Write out what this relationship looks like for you—not what you have been told to want, but what your body and spirit crave. Can you allow this vision to guide your choices? Can you release what does not align with this deeper truth? If parts of you feel unworthy of such love, name them—not to shame them, but to begin healing them. These parts often learned that safety came through self-sacrifice. You are now allowed to teach them something new. You may not yet have this relationship in your life, or perhaps it exists only in fragments. But your ability to name it makes it real. It becomes a boundary, a standard, a vision to grow toward. You are not too much for the love you seek. The connection you long for is not fantasy—it is instruction. It shows you what home feels like, and teaches you how to return to yourself.

Offer gratitude for your inner wisdom—the part of you that still knows what kind of love you deserve. What has this vision revealed about your genuine needs, and how can you thank yourself for no longer settling for less than that?

_____

_____

_____

_____

_____

_____

_____

_____

_____

_____

_____

_____

_____

_____

_____

_____

_____

_____

_____

_____

_____

_____

_____

_____

DAY 20

Buried, not broken—

a dream whispers through the dust,

still asking to bloom.

Some dreams do not live loudly. They do not demand your full attention, nor do they plead for validation. Instead, they rest in the corners of your longing—tender, unproven, waiting. They wait, not because they are weak, but because they know that the timing of becoming matters. Perhaps you have carried one like this. A vision of a different way of living. A story half-told. A truth you once glimpsed but could never fully name. A way of living, working, or loving that once flickered into view and never fully left. What dream have you tucked away—not because it stopped mattering, but because the world did not seem to have space for it? What part of your truth did you sideline to survive, to fit in, to be accepted? Trace its origin. When did you first feel its presence? What kind of version of you was brave enough to imagine it? *What has this dream taught you about who you are?* Maybe it is shaped by your values, the way you see others, the work you choose to do even when no one is watching. Understand this: a dream does not need to be realized in public to be real. It doesn't need validation to be worthy. It only needs to be honored in how you live. Write what this dream still asks of you. Is it patience? Effort? A new kind of risk? Does it want you to speak more honestly? To protect your energy? To start again where you once stopped? You do not need to launch it into the world today. You do not need to build a life around it tomorrow. But could you nourish it in some small, consistent way? Even if that nourishment looks like belief. Even if it looks like not giving up on the parts of yourself that still ache to try. Because not all dreams thunder forward. Some whisper. Some wait. Some become more real simply because you no longer pretend they don't matter.

What has this dream shown you about your inner truth—and how can you offer thanks for the ways it has kept you aligned, inspired, and connected to what matters most, even when it asked for more than you could give?

_____

_____

_____

_____

_____

_____

_____

_____

_____

_____

_____

_____

_____

_____

_____

_____

_____

_____

_____

_____

_____

_____

_____

DAY 21

The door stayed untouched—

but today, your hand found it.

One step changed the air.

There is a certain weight that comes with carrying a hope for too long. It gathers dust, then doubt. You wonder if you've outgrown it—or if it has outgrown you. You question whether it is naïve, too late, or too much. But within that heaviness, something remarkably alive lives—an ember that refuses to go out, no matter how long it has waited, no matter how quiet its flame has become.

Think of one hope you have carried—something not yet realized, but deeply yours. What is one action, however small or unsteady, you have taken toward it? Not the entire journey, just the first courageous reach: signing your name, telling the truth, beginning again after the silence. That step matters. It breaks inertia. It declares to the world— and more importantly, to yourself—that your longing is worthy of movement. Now look at that moment closely. What did you have to overcome to take that step? Whose voice did you have to quiet? What fear did you walk with anyway? Write about what this step cost you—and what it returned. Did it shift something into your body? Did it offer a breath of relief? A glimpse of clarity? Did it stir something in your body—a rising, a settling, a quiet yes? Even if nothing visible has changed, your relationship with the dream has changed. That is not small. That is not nothing. Let yourself name the courage it took to move from holding a hope to honoring it. What might the next step be—not the perfect one, but the truest? One that reflects where you are now, not where you think you should be. How will you sustain your movement without demanding immediate arrival? Dreams that bloom slowly lose none of their beauty. Some roots grow downward long before the blossom appears. Power lies in each tender beginning, even when readiness hasn't yet arrived. Even when belief feels like a whisper. Begin anyway

What part of you trusted your long-held hope enough to move toward it—and how can you express gratitude for the courage that made your beginning possible?

_____

_____

_____

_____

_____

_____

_____

_____

_____

_____

_____

_____

_____

_____

_____

_____

_____

_____

_____

_____

_____

_____

_____

_____

Weekly Practice

Choose to learn something new this week—not to perfect it, but to explore it with curiosity. Let yourself be a beginner: try a new recipe, learn a phrase in another language, tend a plant, sketch a simple scene that catches your eye. Let the learning be small, simple, and sincere. Notice your inner voice—does it rush to judgment, whisper critiques, crave mastery? Or does it open to play, to wonder, to possibility? Each mistake is an invitation to stay kind, to remain open. Growth does not always feel graceful. It stumbles, spills, and starts over. But it always expands your capacity, your imagination, your courage. Reflect on how it felt to do something unfamiliar. Did joy visit in unexpected moments? Did frustration offer insight? What emerged in the space between 'trying' and 'succeeding'? Learning is not just about what you gain—it is who you become in the process when you allow imperfection, when you stay in the room with yourself, when you choose effort over avoidance and exploration over achievement.

The act of learning, in its gentlest form, is a kind of love.

DAY 22

Breath writes quiet songs—

tales of fear, ease, and stillness,

woven through the day.

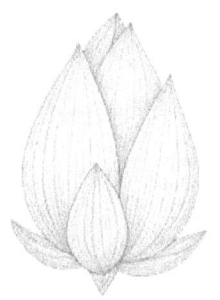

Long before the thought arrives, the breath is already telling the story—rising in haste when fear approaches, halting at surprise, or lengthening in moments of trust. The body speaks in inhales and exhales, and the breath becomes its first language. Begin by listening, not to change it, but to hear what it is trying to say. Throughout the day, pause and notice: Is your breath shallow or full? Fast or hesitant? Does it drift upward into your chest, or anchor downward into your belly? Without keeping score, notice what was happening at that moment—who were you with? What were you feeling? Let these small observations become a kind of map, tracing the contours of your emotional landscape through the simple act of noticing. When do you feel most at home in your breath? Which places or people allow you to breathe without effort, and which take the air from you? This is not a project of control, but a practice of trust—learning the language of your body's whisper before it becomes a scream. The body will always tell you the truth—it just needs you to listen without rushing past the message. With time, you will recognize the breath not just as a function, but as a wise and faithful companion.

What softened inside you, and what made that space feel safe enough to breathe deeply?

_____

_____

_____

_____

_____

_____

_____

_____

_____

_____

_____

_____

_____

_____

_____

_____

_____

_____

_____

_____

_____

_____

_____

DAY 23

Exhale like soft rain,

washing fear from hidden rooms—

quiet returns home.

The breath out—the release—is where the softest kind of power lives. It carries within it a message of safety, a gentle affirmation that your body no longer needs to brace itself. When the world feels too sharp, too close, or too loud, it draws your awareness to exhale, not as an escape, but as a way of signaling to your body that it no longer needs to guard. Inhale slowly through your nose for a slow count of four, letting the air travel deep into your belly. Then exhale through parted lips for six or more, as though fogging a glass in slow motion. Let the breath pour out not in haste, but in devotion. Let this rhythm repeat three to five times, especially when your body begins to brace or your thoughts rush ahead. You may place one hand on your chest or abdomen, not to control, but to feel yourself staying. With each exhale, whisper a steadying phrase: "I am safe here." or "Nothing else is required right now." Let your words nest within your breath, carrying comfort to where it's needed most. Notice if your shoulders descend, if your jaw loosens, if space returns to your ribs. This is not a trick; it is the body remembering itself through care. The longer breath out becomes a thread of return—a subtle tether leading you back to center. It is kind, and real. And it is always available, even in the thickest moments of uncertainty.

What did you learn about your ability to soothe and support yourself from within?

_____

_____

_____

_____

_____

_____

_____

_____

_____

_____

_____

_____

_____

_____

_____

_____

_____

_____

_____

_____

_____

_____

_____

_____

DAY 24

Breath weaves morning light,

soft curtains draw and unfold—

day begins and ends.

Before the rush of the day or as evening settles, the breath holds a sacred power to shape your experience. It is a quiet force—steady, faithful—ready to ground you in moments of transition. Create a simple ritual: find a place where you can sit, perhaps beside a window where light drifts or near a plant, a candle, a space that feels soft. This isn't about atmosphere—it's about belonging to the moment. Rest one hand on your chest, the other on your belly, and let your inhale glide through your nose, tracing its path downward. Exhale through parted lips, like a whispered candle flame fading, slow and intentional. Repeat this cycle five times, allowing the breath to become a gentle unfolding rather than a task. Then ask yourself with sincerity: What energy do you wish to invite into your day? What are you ready to let go of—a tension, worry, or expectation? Let this ritual serve as a promise to yourself—a reaffirmation of your presence here, in this hour, on this earth. Over time, it will not be just breath, but a tender doorway—a coming home to your own inner landscape, a place where you no longer need to perform, where awareness and kindness gently meet.

How did your breath welcome or close day?

_____

_____

_____

_____

_____

_____

_____

_____

_____

_____

_____

_____

_____

_____

_____

_____

_____

_____

_____

_____

_____

_____

_____

_____

DAY 25

No screen between us—

your eyes met mine, and time slowed.

We were truly here.

To be present with another is a rare and sacred act. Not just physically near, but fully engaged—unscattered, unrushed, unattached to what comes next. It is a quiet rebellion against the fragmentation of modern life. In a world that constantly pulls your attention outward, offering someone your undivided presence is an offering of the highest kind. It says: "I am here with you. Not multitasking. Not half-listening. But choosing this moment fully." And perhaps more importantly, it is a practice of returning to your own life as it unfolds, breath by breath, word by word. Think of the last time you were with someone and felt entirely in it—not halfway listening, not calculating your reply, not reaching for your phone out of habit. What made that connection feel anchored? What allowed you to stop performing and start witnessing? What habits or fears tend to pull you away from the moment? Is it discomfort with silence? A need to stay productive? The impulse to avoid intimacy or unpredictability? Choose one conversation today where you will put the phone away—not in your lap, not on the table, but out of reach. Let your body turn fully toward the other person—your shoulders, your gaze, your attention. Pay attention to the rhythm of their voice, the pause between their sentences, and the expression behind their words. Listen, not to respond, but to understand. It may feel vulnerable, even unsettling, to be this present. But within that discomfort is an opening—a chance to truly meet another human being without a filter. And in doing so, you also meet yourself. Actual connection does not demand grandeur; it asks only for your presence. This is how trust grows. This is how intimacy deepens. This is how you remember that life is happening now, not in the scroll, the schedule, or the next obligation. But here. In breath. In witness. In shared being.

Recall a recent moment where you set distraction aside and gave someone your full attention. What did that exchange awaken in you? How can you thank yourself for choosing to stay with what was real and unfolding, right in front of you?

_____

_____

_____

_____

_____

_____

_____

_____

_____

_____

_____

_____

_____

_____

_____

_____

_____

_____

_____

_____

_____

_____

_____

DAY 26

Your name still echoes—

not always with warmth, but truth.

You carved part of me.

Some relationships leave a lasting imprint—not because they lasted forever, but because they touched something primal and foundational within us. They cracked us open or held a mirror to the pieces we hadn't yet seen. Whether marked by love, loss, rupture, or revelation, these connections shape the person you have become. To revisit them now is not an attempt to reopen the wound, but to understand the scar. To trace its edge with curiosity, not judgment. This reflection is not about dwelling; it's about listening for what still lingers. Because sometimes, what remains has more to teach us than what once was. Choose one relationship from your past that still lives within you. It might be a parent, a friend, a lover, a teacher—someone who either offered you a version of yourself you did not know existed or fractured something you have since had to rebuild. Write their name. Without judgment, list what they taught you—not what they intended, but what you learned in the aftermath. What beliefs about love, trust, worth, or boundaries were formed in their presence? Which of those beliefs still shape the way you relate today—and which no longer serve you? This reflection is not about assigning blame. It is about seeing clearly. If there is grief, let it surface. If there is gratitude, let that live alongside the grief. You are allowed to feel both. Consider writing a letter you will not send—offering the words you never spoke, or reclaiming the voice you once silenced. What would you have said if you felt fully safe? What truth wants to rise now, after all this time? Relationships do not have to be ongoing to be influential. And those that harmed you do not get to define you forever. You are allowed to grow beyond them—and to carry what was beautiful without guilt. You get to decide what stays, and what you now release. Not because it wasn't real, but because you are ready to live unbound.

Think of the relationship that shaped you most profoundly. What strength, clarity, or self-understanding did you gain through that connection—and how can you thank yourself for surviving, growing, or softening in the ways it asked of you?

_____

_____

_____

_____

_____

_____

_____

_____

_____

_____

_____

_____

_____

_____

_____

_____

_____

_____

_____

_____

_____

_____

_____

_____

DAY 27

Eyes wide like morning—

a question stirs the still air,

the world leans closer.

Curiosity is not always loud. It can arrive as a pulse, a pull, a flicker of interest that interrupts routine with a breath of aliveness. Wonder, too, is often wordless—arising not from answers but from permission to not yet know. What draws you in, not for gain or praise, but because it stirs your spirit awake? Where in your life do you feel most alive with questions? These are not always grand or noble pursuits—they might live in the way light lands on water, the behavior of birds, how a stranger holds grief in their eyes, or the mystery behind the recurring dreams of a certain place. Curiosity speaks through the things you linger over without effort, through the things you chase late into the night for no reason except that they matter to your heart. Make a list of three things that capture your interest again and again. What do these have in common? What do they awaken in you? Wonder is often a mirror—it reflects what we value, what we hunger to understand, and sometimes, what we long to heal. Now write about how you might make more space for these sparks. Do they want more time? Structure? Freedom? Are they asking to be shared, or held close for now? How might you honor these questions without rushing to tame them? You do not have to know where your wonder will lead in order to trust its importance. Its value isn't in its destination but in the way it invites you to be more present, more porous, more human.

What are you most thankful for in your relationship with curiosity—and how can you show reverence for the things that ignite your wonder, asking nothing of you but to be fully engaged and wholly human?

_____

_____

_____

_____

_____

_____

_____

_____

_____

_____

_____

_____

_____

_____

_____

_____

_____

_____

_____

_____

_____

_____

_____

_____

DAY 28

Dust does not mean death —

beneath it, something still glows,

waiting for your hand.

There may be something you once loved that faded—not from lack of meaning, but from the weight of everything else. Responsibilities pressed in. Time narrowed. Doubt whispered: "What is the point?" And so, the thing you once grasped—be it drawing, dancing, languages, woodwork, music, movement, invention—was laid aside. Not erased but buried. Yet even neglected fires can reignite. What is one passion you have left behind, not because it ceased to matter, but because life moved too quickly to carry it? Try tracing its imprint. How did it shape who you were? What kind of aliveness did it give you? If you close your eyes, can you remember the feeling it stirred up with, the particular kind of joy that had no audience, no agenda? What would it take to revisit that spark? Not to master it. Not to monetize it. Simply to touch the thread of who you were when it mattered most. Maybe it begins with ten minutes a week. Maybe you let yourself be a beginner again, especially if you once held yourself to impossible standards. Let it be a reconnection, not a resumption. You are not returning to who you were—you are meeting this love with who you are now. What passion does this need from you to survive this season of life? Space? Playfulness? Patience? And what might it offer in return? Joy. Centering. A reminder that you are more than what the world demands of you. You don't have to perfect it. You only need to say: I still remember you.

What do you feel grateful for having once loved something—and how might you honor that love now, by choosing to let even a small piece of it live again in your present life?

_____

_____

_____

_____

_____

_____

_____

_____

_____

_____

_____

_____

_____

_____

_____

_____

_____

_____

_____

_____

_____

_____

Be gentle first with wounds your heart has grown,
For every soul walks paths not fully known.
A tender word, to self or stranger cast,
Can bloom in places cold and overgrown.

What treasure lies in gold or earned acclaim,
If kindness flickers like a dying flame?
But give with grace, not counting what returns—
And find your joy no wealth could ever claim.

Forgive yourself the times you lost your way,
The stumbles made when skies had turned to gray.
Each fault, a teacher—each regret, a seed—
That blooms when shame is gently swept away.

And when you pardon others from the heart,
You set your soul and theirs a world apart.
For mercy given is a mirror too—
It frees the giver as much as the marked.

Weekly Practice

This week, bring your intention to enter conversations as a witness rather than a responder. Resist the pull to fix, explain, or interrupt. Instead, when someone speaks, stay with their words. Watch their face. Hear not just the story, but the feeling underneath. Let your presence be a quiet container where others can unfold without fear. When it is your turn to speak, pause. Let your response come from understanding, not reaction. Even a few moments of deep, attuned listening can soften the edges of a relationship, transforming it from transactional to transformational. This is not passive—it is an active, intentional kind of attention—the kind that asks you to hold space, rather than fill it. And in doing so, you offer something rare: the grace of being truly seen.

DAY 29

No tools in my hands—

just the open space to hear

what aches without cure.

There is a sacred kind of listening that asks nothing of you but your presence. Not your answers. Not your insights. Not your need to lift the weight from someone else's shoulders. Just your willingness to stay near the truth of another without shrinking from it or reshaping it into something more manageable. This kind of presence doesn't come naturally in a world that prizes answers and urgency. It requires intention. Stillness. Trust. When someone shares their pain or confusion, notice your instinct—do you rush to offer advice, soften their sadness, search for a solution? What part of you feels responsible for their relief? And what might happen if you simply stayed with them in the unknown? True empathy does not always arrive with strategies. It often begins with restraint. By allowing their story to be what it is—unfinished, messy, unresolved. Practice this today. In conversation, resist the urge to insert yourself. Reflect back on what you hear without adding a path forward. You might say, "That sounds really heavy," or, "I can see how deeply that is affecting you." These are not dismissals. They are acknowledgements, and they are powerful. They are affirmations. Tiny gestures that say: I see you. I'm with you. Can you be a mirror instead of a map? Can you witness without rearranging? When you give someone the space to be fully heard, you offer them the dignity of their own process. You say, without words, I trust your wisdom. I believe in your capacity to find your way. And maybe that is what they needed more than anything: not to be rescued, but to be respected. Because there is something profoundly healing in being seen just as you are—with nothing added, nothing taken away.

Think of a time when you held space for someone without stepping in to fix their pain. What did that experience teach you about presence—and how can you thank yourself for offering care that honored their story rather than controlling its shape?

_____

_____

_____

_____

_____

_____

_____

_____

_____

_____

_____

_____

_____

_____

_____

_____

_____

_____

_____

_____

_____

_____

_____

_____

DAY 30

The body remembers—

silent stories curled beneath

skin that longs to speak.

Instead of moving quickly past the edges of discomfort, slow down and listen with presence—begin by scanning your body with attention, as though your hands could hear. Where is the tension gathering—your jaw, your belly, the base of your spine? These are not flaws to be fixed, but signals, carrying stories your mind may have silenced. Each ache, each clench, may carry history: fear tucked away, boundaries crossed, grief that never found a name. Is this fear? A shield? A grief I have not named? Speak to the sensation with honesty: "This is bracing," or "This is holding something sacred." Let your body hear that it's not wrong to feel. That its signals are welcome. Then, soften the posture—unclench the jaw, rest your shoulders, breathe warmth into the space. Allow your body to be both witness and guide—trust that it holds truths that may take time to unfold. The healing begins not in changing the sensation, but in staying with it, without hurry. Over time, this practice becomes a language of safety, a way of returning home to yourself with compassion.

Offer gratitude for your body's wisdom—for the way it carries, protects, and signals when you need care. What has your body taught you today by allowing you to feel?

_____

_____

_____

_____

_____

_____

_____

_____

_____

_____

_____

_____

_____

_____

_____

_____

_____

_____

_____

_____

_____

_____

_____

_____

_____

DAY 31

The body whispers

in arcs, spirals, subtle sway—

truth moves without words.

Allow your body to take the lead today, not to perform, but to express. Stand or sit without a plan, and begin to shift your weight—left, then right. Roll your shoulders as if shedding layers you forgot you were carrying. Trace the air with your hands like they're remembering something long forgotten. What gestures feel like a sigh from within? Like a return to your own rhythm? Let go of how it should look and instead ask yourself, what does your body want to say to you that your words cannot? Stretch if you need space, shake if energy feels trapped, or sway if stillness feels too tight. Move with care enough to notice the subtle shifts—how tension melts, how breath finds its way back in. This is not about form, but about re-inhabiting yourself with care. Let each motion remind you that your body is not something to fix, but something to listen to. Notice how the rhythm of intuitive movement softens your thoughts and creates space for emotions to be felt, with no need to be solved. This is not a practice of control, but of communion—with yourself, through movement.

What did you learn from your body by listening through motion instead of words?

_____

_____

_____

_____

_____

_____

_____

_____

_____

_____

_____

_____

_____

_____

_____

_____

_____

_____

_____

_____

_____

_____

_____

_____

_____

_____

DAY 32

I release the plea—

no need for every soul to share

the truth of my being.

There comes a point when the burden of constant explanation fades into unnecessary weight. We grow used to clarifying ourselves in the hope of acceptance, polishing our experiences into digestible pieces for others. You might notice an urge to confirm your worth through the eyes of others, yet this need only serves as a veil over your true self. Identify a recent moment when you felt compelled to clarify your stance or feelings, even when silence would have sufficed. Write what you wished you could have simply been rather than explained. Ask yourself: Is my value contingent on being fully understood by everyone? Notice if any part of you fears that being misunderstood might lead to rejection. Challenge that assumption by listing ways in which misunderstanding allowed you to grow or discover new truths. Define one situation where you will choose to share simply—without the pressure of validation or explanation—and observe what shifts within you. Commit to honoring your authenticity by practicing concise self-expression, even if it feels raw or exposed. Reflect on what it might look like to live with the certainty that some minds may never capture all you are, yet that remains perfectly acceptable. Consider journaling your feelings when vulnerability emerges, noting specifically the instances when explaining less made you feel more empowered. Confront the notion that every soul needs to see you in complete clarity for you to stand firmly in your own truth. Reframe misunderstanding as a natural occurrence that fosters your independence rather than diminishes your value. Explore what life could look like if you relinquish the quest for universal understanding and instead nurture your own insight. Let this release open a doorway to deeper self-compassion—a recognition that your being is enough without universal approval.

Reflect on a time when you embraced being partially known by someone yet still felt whole. What aspects of that experience can you celebrate, and how might you express gratitude for the freedom that comes with accepting that not every heart needs to fully decode you?

_____

_____

_____

_____

_____

_____

_____

_____

_____

_____

_____

_____

_____

_____

_____

_____

_____

_____

_____

_____

_____

_____

DAY 33

Rooted in the earth,

body whispers calm and strength—

storm fades into still.

When the mind spins beyond its borders and overwhelms your breath, turn carefully to the physical world you carry within. Turn gently toward the landscape of your physical self—the world within that asks only to be felt, not solved. Sense the firm weight of your feet connecting with the floor, the way your body settles into the chair's embrace. These sensations are not distractions. They are invitations. Anchors. Let these sensations become your refuge—steady points in the swirling storm of thought. Explore grounding with intention: press your palms together, turn into the subtle rhythm of your pulse beneath your wrists, or imagine thick roots unfurling from your feet deep into the nourishing earth. Let your body's connection to the ground speak its own language of safety and clarity. How does this steady presence shift the tension inside you? Notice if calm blooms like a slow unfolding, how sharper edges soften and focus returns without force. Revisit this practice whenever your thoughts scatter or decisions loom large, allowing grounding to grow into a companion—a strength you carry beneath the surface. Over time, this rooted steadiness will become a sanctuary, holding space for softness and resilience in equal parts.

What aspects of your body's peace are you grateful for today, and how has this strength helped you embrace uncertainty with courage?

_____

_____

_____

_____

_____

_____

_____

_____

_____

_____

_____

_____

_____

_____

_____

_____

_____

_____

_____

_____

_____

_____

_____

_____

DAY 34

I held back my edge —

and saw, behind their defense,

a wound not unlike mine.

It is easy to extend compassion to those who meet you with grace. It flows naturally when you feel safe, understood, and welcomed. But the real invitation arises in the presence of someone who triggers discomfort—whose words cut too sharp, or whose presence seems to demand more than you wish to give. These are often the moments when compassion holds its greatest power—not for them, but for you. It liberates you from reactivity and allows you to choose your response with integrity and care.

Begin with honesty. Who tests your patience, empathy, or calm? Write their name. Instead of rehearsing what frustrates you, ask: What might this person carry that I cannot see? What pain might live beneath their posture of control, distance, or irritation? This isn't about excusing harm or abandoning boundaries. On the contrary, it is about discerning with compassion. It means shifting the question from what is wrong with them to what might have happened to them. Then, turn inward. What parts of you feel threatened, unseen, or dismissed in their presence? Trace that feeling—not to shame it, but to understand what it mirrors in you. Sometimes, the ones we resist most reflect something unresolved within us. Practice one compassionate act in your next interaction. It could be a pause before reacting, a softened tone, or an inner reminder: They are human, too. Hold your boundary and your heart. Both can coexist. Compassion does not always change the other. Sometimes, it changes the lens through which you carry them. And through that, you reclaim your peace from their chaos.

Think of the person who has stretched your emotional capacity the most. What strength, awareness, or self-respect have you gained by practicing compassion in their presence— and how can you offer yourself gratitude for staying open without losing yourself?

_____

_____

_____

_____

_____

_____

_____

_____

_____

_____

_____

_____

_____

_____

_____

_____

_____

_____

_____

_____

_____

_____

_____

_____

DAY 35

Sky without a map—

the dream drifts where it wishes,

unburdened by end.

Not every dream needs a deadline. Some dreams come not to be measured, some arrive to remind you what it means to be alive—curious, expansive, and untethered from constant striving. Yet, in a culture obsessed with outcomes, even dreaming can become a performance: tracked, measured, and judged. You might ask, "What will this become?" before you even allow the dream to speak. But what if dreaming is allowed to be an experience, not a transaction? What if you gave yourself a pocket of time where no one asks for proof or progress, including you? Can you name a longing that still lives in you, even if it is vague or tender or unfinished? Write it down. Speak it aloud. Not to fix it, but to give it breath. Now imagine what it might feel like to give that dream room to stretch without expectation. Could you dedicate part of your week to wandering— creatively, imaginatively, with no need to arrive? Could you try a practice that feels aimless, yet freeing—journaling without a topic, sketching without skill, planning a trip you may never take? Notice where pressure creeps in. Whose voice does it carry? What story does it tell about worth? Write back to that voice in one sentence: "This dream does not owe anyone anything." Let this be your invitation to dream for the sake of dreaming. To explore for the sake of wonder. To build a relationship with the part of you that still believes in possibility—on your own terms, in your own time.

What do you feel thankful for in your ability to imagine beyond what is, and how might you express gratitude for the space—however small—you are creating to let your dreams breathe, without asking them to perform?

_____

_____

_____

_____

_____

_____

_____

_____

_____

_____

_____

_____

_____

_____

_____

_____

_____

_____

_____

_____

_____

_____

_____

_____

Weekly Practice

Each day this week, offer a gesture of kindness, expecting nothing in return. This could be holding the door, paying for someone's coffee, picking up litter, or leaving a kind note for a stranger. Let the act be simple, sincere, and quiet. Do it even when no one is watching. Let giving become a rhythm of your day, not for praise, but for connection. Notice how it shifts your relationship with the world. Does your heart feel softer? Do your eyes seek more gently? Kindness is not a performance—it is an orientation, a way of moving through the world with open hands. It is how you choose to exist within the ordinary moments, creating space where connection might gently bloom.

Lavender

DAY 36

Their voice, thin with doubt—

I looked, and did not look through

They softened, and stayed.

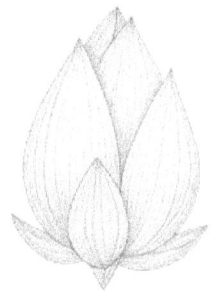

Some souls drift through this world like shadows cast at dusk—not because they are hiding, but because others have stopped looking. They move through the margins, quietly carrying stories that have never been invited into the light. Their pain becomes background noise. Their joy is rarely asked about. They speak and are not heard, or are only half-heard, spoken over, dismissed. And often, they begin to shrink in response— not out of weakness, but as a quiet defense.

A way to preserve what is sacred when the world forgets to be gentle. This is not a weakness. It is what resilience sometimes looks like when it must retreat. Think about someone in your orbit—at work, in your family, your community—whose presence tends to be overlooked. Not because you do not care, but because their voice does not demand attention. When was the last time you slowed enough to truly witness them? What might they be carrying that no one else has asked about? What untold joys they cradle. What quiet strength has gone unspoken.

Offering your presence is not about fixing or rescuing—it is about choosing to stay. It means engaging without distraction, listening without rehearsing your reply, and noticing without interpreting. It could look like asking a second question when they give you a short answer. Or remembering something they once shared and circling back to it later. It could mean saying, "I see you," with no need for them to prove they deserve it.

This practice is not performative—it is intimate, and at times, uncomfortable. It invites you to sit beside someone else's quiet ache or unnoticed strength. It requires you to resist the impulse to overlook what is unfamiliar or inconvenient. In doing so, you remind them—and yourself—that presence is power. That attention, when freely offered, becomes a kind of belonging. And sometimes, your willingness to see someone fully becomes the moment they begin to return to themselves. Piece by quiet piece.

Think of someone you have truly seen—not out of duty, but from a place of genuine presence. What shifted in that interaction, and how can you thank yourself for offering your time and attention as a form of gentle care?

_____

_____

_____

_____

_____

_____

_____

_____

_____

_____

_____

_____

_____

_____

_____

_____

_____

_____

_____

DAY 37

No name, yet I see—

your eyes carry stories too.

We are not apart.

Compassion for strangers asks something quietly radical of us: to love without shared history, without the safety net of reciprocity. It is love untethered to obligation, stripped of narrative, resting solely on the recognition that beneath all the roles and masks, we share the same human ache. The same fragile longing to be seen. When you pass someone on the street, sit beside them on the train, or brush briefly into their day— what would shift if you imagined their pain as real as yours? What if the man slumped on the bench, the woman lost in thought at the crosswalk, the child staring blankly into the crowd were carrying wounds that mirror your own? It is easy to harden. Easy to dismiss the unknown, to stay safe behind the armor of detachment. But sacred love begins where assumptions end. When you choose to see another person, not as an inconvenience or background, but as someone carrying invisible weight, you create a fracture in indifference. That fracture matters. It softens what the world has hardened. Where do you withhold kindness out of habit or fear? What judgments do you default to when you do not understand someone's way of being? Next time on the street, choose one stranger—someone you pass without pause—and pause. Not to fix, not to speak, but to see. You might offer a nod, a held door, or simply a silent blessing. These gestures will not change their entire life, but they may shift yours. They are reminders that connection does not require words or names—only willingness. This kind of compassion is radical because it refuses the idea that love must be earned. His life matters to you, even if you do not know his name. When enough people hold that truth, the world softens—not in sentiment, but in structure. Practice this not just once, but often. Let it become the lens through which you engage, especially when your instinct is to look away.

When did you offer unexpected kindness to someone? What did that moment awaken in you—and how can you thank yourself for loving with no need to be asked, or even acknowledged?

_____

_____

_____

_____

_____

_____

_____

_____

_____

_____

_____

_____

_____

_____

_____

_____

_____

_____

_____

_____

_____

DAY 38

Out of nowhere, light—

a hand reached, uninvited,

and everything stilled.

Some forms of kindness slip into our lives like sunlight through a half-closed curtain—gentle, unbidden, and transformative. The one that lingers longest often arrives from a stranger, asking nothing, expecting nothing. No shared history, no reason to pause—but they did. And in that pause, something inside you softened. Perhaps you were struggling in silence, not yet ready to name your pain. Perhaps your defenses were high, and their warmth slipped through anyway. Think back. Who surprised you with care when you did not ask for it? What gesture broke through your aloneness—a stranger's word, an offer of help, a moment of being seen in your invisibility? Let yourself return to that moment, not as a story, but as a sensation. The way your breath shifted. The way your shoulders eased. The way your heart, briefly, was held. Something changed in that moment. What changed in you when you realized someone chose to care, not out of obligation, but out of instinct? Why did that moment stay with you? What need did it meet, what belief did it quietly challenge? Maybe it reminded you that you are not as alone as you once believed. Maybe it marked a turning point—a reminder that good things can come unannounced. Write what their action taught you about how you want to move through the world. Could you offer that same unexpected presence to someone else? Not as performance, but as inheritance—passing forward the healing you once received. Let this memory become a thread in the fabric of how you live: simple, unforced, but powerful in its timing. Let it guide your presence in the lives of others. Unexpected kindness reveals a more tender world than we sometimes remember. Let yourself believe that again.

Who offered you kindness when you needed it most—before you could ask, before you had words? How did that gesture shift something inside you?

_____

_____

_____

_____

_____

_____

_____

_____

_____

_____

_____

_____

_____

_____

_____

_____

_____

_____

_____

_____

_____

_____

_____

DAY 39

Tired bones hum low notes,

a quiet plea wrapped in breath—

rest is a return.

Fatigue rarely arrives unannounced—it whispers through the weight behind your eyes, the resistance in your limbs, the sigh before another task. Before reaching for distraction or self-judgment, inquire softly, without urgency, what kind of tired are you? Not all weariness is the same. Is your body weary, your heart stretched thin, or your spirit fraying at the edges? Choose rest that speaks directly to that place—perhaps lying down without stimulation, stepping away from obligations, or simply sitting in silence where nothing is expected of you. If your body is weary, let yourself lie down in stillness—not with a screen or a soundtrack, but with space. If your heart is tired, step away from the noise of obligation. Let yourself be unneeded for a while. If your spirit is fraying, find silence where nothing is asked of you. Just be, untethered from doing. If guilt surfaces, name it without shame, and then remind yourself: needing rest does not make you fragile—it makes you human. Your worth does not diminish in stillness. Rest is not the absence of progress, but the soil from which your presence grows. Let today be a soft yes to your body's wisdom, your heart's timing, your soul's pace. Choose the kind of rest that listens—not just to your fatigue, but to what's underneath it.

Because in the quiet of rest, you do not disappear. You begin again.

Offer thanks for the signals your body gives when it needs care. What are you grateful for in the ways your body or spirit asked for rest today—and how you honored that need?

_____

_____

_____

_____

_____

_____

_____

_____

_____

_____

_____

_____

_____

_____

_____

_____

_____

_____

_____

_____

_____

_____

_____

DAY 40

After the long day,

the body forgets its name—

whisper it back home.

After a long day of tension, depletion, or quiet overwhelm, your body may feel distant—unfamiliar in its slowness, uncertain in its response. Instead of asking it to be strong again, offer it your full presence, like sitting beside someone who's just returned from a long journey. You wouldn't demand they rise, smile, and carry on. You'd simply be with them. Offer your body that same grace. Be the companion it's been waiting for. Choose one gentle gesture each day: trace warmth into your hands before placing them over your heart, notice what fabrics feel comforting against your skin, or take a walk without a goal. What would safety feel like in your body right now? Maybe it's stillness. Maybe it's rhythm. Maybe it's space. Let the answer guide how you move, rest, or touch. Your job is not to fix, but to re-establish trust—step by step, without rushing. If irritation or disappointment surfaces, name them, then return with tenderness; healing often moves in circles, not straight lines. You do not have to feel restored to live with care. You only have to begin again, right where you are. Speak to your body as you would to someone precious: "Thank you for carrying me, even when it hurts to do so." In time, your body will remember that it is safe with you. That it is supported. That you are its home.

Offer gratitude for one way your body supported you today, even if it was subtle. What softness or strength did you notice—and how did it help you feel just a little more like yourself?

_____

_____

_____

_____

_____

_____

_____

_____

_____

_____

_____

_____

_____

_____

_____

_____

_____

_____

_____

_____

_____

_____

_____

_____

DAY 41

The wind shifts again—

but deep beneath the surface,

roots still hold their shape.

In a world that pulls your attention in every direction, values are the compass beneath the noise. They are not abstract ideas but living truths that shape your choices—often without applause. Your values emerge in the way you speak up when it's uncomfortable, in how you protect the tender things no one sees, or when you walk away without explanation—because something in your core wouldn't let you stay. Other times, they are buried beneath people-pleasing or fear, waiting to be remembered. When did you recently feel proud—not for being perfect, but for being true to yourself? Was it when you spoke up? When you said "no" to someone you loved, because saying "yes" would have meant abandoning yourself? When you offered kindness—when no one witnessed, but you did it anyway? Trace those moments backward. What value was breathing underneath? Make a list of five values that feel the most present in your life right now. Not what you think should be there, but what truly is—integrity, freedom, presence, justice, creativity, care, rest, devotion. Where are these values honored in your daily life? Where are they dismissed or betrayed? The gap between your values and your actions can feel like friction or fatigue—pay attention to those signals. This is not about judgment. It is about alignment. Where could you adjust the rhythm of your days to make more space for what matters most? Even small shifts in speech, routine, or attention can serve as declarations of your truth. Your values are not stagnant—they grow as you do. But when you name them, they become the thread that connects who you are, who you have been, and who you are becoming. Let that thread guide you through the noise. It already knows the way.

What are you grateful for in the values that guide your life—and how can you thank the part of you that keeps choosing what matters, even when it is hard, even when no one else sees?

_____

_____

_____

_____

_____

_____

_____

_____

_____

_____

_____

_____

_____

_____

_____

_____

_____

_____

_____

_____

_____

_____

_____

DAY 42

Not every whisper

is meant to be ignored—

some carry your true name.

There is a subtle but profound difference between urgency and importance, but it can be difficult to discern it in a world wired for noise. Urgency taps at your window, loud and insistent, demanding attention with flashing lights and endless notifications. It makes you feel like if you don't act now, everything will slip away. Importance, on the other hand, waits patiently beneath the surface. It hums—not to be ignored, but not in a rush. It doesn't clamor, it calls. Do they reflect what matters most to you? Notice where your energy goes out of obligation and where it moves with devotion. What pulls you back into alignment—with no need to be loud or dramatic? It could be a value you keep returning to, like a favorite melody, a longing that won't let go, no matter how many times you try to quiet it, or an insistence that whispers, there is more than this. The call of what matters often does not scream. It hums beneath the surface, waiting for your willingness to listen. Where do you feel most like yourself? What practices or people help you return to your center? Let yourself feel what anchors your days—not as a weight to carry, but as a truth to hold. These are clues. What decisions have you made recently that were rooted in meaning rather than fear? Which ones felt hollow, even if they looked impressive? The call of what truly matters often asks you to disappoint someone—maybe even your past self—to honor who you are now. It can sting. But alignment doesn't always come with applause. It comes with truth. And truth often asks you to be brave in silence. Are you willing to let that be okay? Are you willing to listen even when it complicates your plans? You do not need to figure it all out today. But you need to listen. Begin again by naming one thing that matters to you more than being liked, more than being right, more than being safe. Let it lead—not with force, but with fidelity. Not with fear, but with tenderness. That one thread can begin to weave the life you're truly meant to live.

What are you thankful for in your capacity to hear the truth beneath the noise—and how might you honor your gratitude by living in alignment with what matters, even if just in one area of your life today?

_____

_____

_____

_____

_____

_____

_____

_____

_____

_____

_____

_____

_____

_____

_____

_____

_____

_____

_____

_____

_____

_____

Weekly Practice

Open space for someone—yourself included—and write a letter of forgiveness. Let the words come without editing, without needing to be eloquent or fair. Speak what hurts, and then name what you are ready to release. You do not need to send this letter. It is not for anybody else—it is for your healing. Set it aside in a drawer or burn it with care. As the letter leaves your hand, notice what softens in your chest. Forgiveness does not erase pain; it simply stops asking it to define you. This act is not about forgetting—it is about unburdening the heart so it can beat more freely.

DAY 43

If you were my friend,

I would hold you without condition—

why not do the same?

You know how to comfort others. You've held their trembling truths like glass, careful not to press too hard or pull away too soon. You have wrapped their shame in understanding, their regrets in warmth. With tenderness that seems to arrive before judgment can speak, you've whispered words like, "You did your best." " You could not have known." "You do not deserve to carry this forever." And when their voices shake with the weight of guilt, you offer grace without hesitation. And yet when it comes to your own mistakes, your voice sharpens. You revisit the moment again and again, as if pain alone could atone for it. You play back scenes from your past again and again, rehearsing remorse as if it might rewrite the story. If your closest friend confessed the very thing you carry shame over, what would you say to him? Write that out in detail. Intone it, as if it were sacred truth—because it is. Notice the double standard: the way you extend grace outward but deny it inward. The way you offer compassion like oxygen to those gasping for breath, but deny yourself even a sip. What part of you still believes forgiveness must be earned through suffering? That healing must be painful, and mercy must be reserved? But forgiveness is not the same as forgetting. It is not letting yourself off the hook without growth. It is releasing the grip of judgment so healing can begin. It's about unclenching your fists—not to discard accountability, but to cradle it with honesty and care. Choose one part of yourself you have struggled to forgive yourself, maybe a choice you regret, a version of yourself you have outgrown, or a truth you have ignored too long. Name it clearly. What lesson did it carry? What did you learn by living through that? Write yourself a letter—not with excuses, but with understanding. Begin with: You were trying to survive the best you knew how. End with: I release you now. Let this become your practice—to meet your wounds not only with accountability, but with mercy. The same mercy you offer others when they fall. Let it belong to you too. You don't need to be punished to be redeemed. You just need to be seen—with softness, with truth, with love that doesn't flinch.

Revisit the memory of choosing compassion over justice, when someone stood before you in their brokenness—and you did not turn away. What made you give it? Now turn inward—what part of yourself is asking for that same compassion, and how can you thank yourself for learning to offer it not only outward, but homeward too?

_____

_____

_____

_____

_____

_____

_____

_____

_____

_____

_____

_____

_____

_____

_____

_____

DAY 44

I heard the harsh voice—

then asked, "Whose words are these, truly?"

The silence answered.

A voice lives inside you—rising of its own will, unasked and undeniable. It critiques, corrects, condemns—sometimes in words you've inherited but never questioned. Often, it echoes someone else: a parent, a teacher, a culture that equated worth with perfection. And in moments of vulnerability—when you're tired, when you've stumbled, when you're exposed. It tightens its grip with quiet cruelty: You are not doing enough. You should know better. What is wrong with you? Listen for the hush before it speaks—the voice that threads itself into your inner world. Not just what it says, but what triggers it. When do you hear it loudest? Is it when you fall behind? When you make a mistake? When you feel exposed? Write down the last thing you silently told yourself in judgment. Would you say this to a friend who is trying their best? The answer matters. You do not need to drown out the voice with forced positivity. You only need to interrupt its momentum. When the inner critic speaks, pause and ask yourself what you truly need right now? Often, beneath the harshness, there's a buried longing—not for perfection but for safety, for love, for enoughness. Respond to that need instead of the accusation. Even a whispered phrase like "This is hard, and I am still learning" can shift the tone. A whisper of grace can echo louder than a shout of shame. Consider writing one phrase you will use when your inner dialogue spirals. Make it real. Make it believable. Make it yours. Something you can believe, even if only halfway, like: "I do not need to earn my worth through flawlessness." Repetition builds familiarity. Familiarity builds trust. This practice is not about becoming endlessly kind to yourself overnight. It is about creating enough space between the wound and the weapon so that you stop turning one into the other. You are allowed to be imperfect and still deserving. You are allowed to unlearn the voices that never spoke with love. You are allowed, simply and fully, to be free.

Return to that flicker of when you stood at the edge of self-judgment, and chose, instead, a gentler way. What did that shift feel like, and how can you thank yourself for beginning to change the way you speak to the person who lives within you?

_____

_____

_____

_____

_____

_____

_____

_____

_____

_____

_____

_____

_____

_____

_____

_____

_____

_____

_____

_____

_____

_____

_____

DAY 45

Stillness hides the thorn—

beneath what I have let go lies

what I have not released.

Resentment is often misunderstood. It's framed as a flaw, a failure in character, something to be suppressed or ignored. But beneath its sharp edges, resentment is a signal. It rises when something within you has been denied, dismissed, or unmet. It may disguise itself as apathy or cynicism. It may cloak itself in sarcasm or silence. But at its core, resentment holds a wounded hope—a version of you that longed to be heard, valued, protected. When you tell yourself you have "moved on," yet bitterness still flashes at the mention of a name, a memory, or a silence—pause. That flash is not a regression. It is a place in your spirit still asking to be met. That is not failure. That is a place still asking for your presence. Where does resentment still live in you? What boundary was crossed, and did you ever acknowledge it—without minimizing? Trace it back, not to blame, but to clarify. Whose choices left you carrying weight they should have held? What part of you keeps rehearsing the injustice as a way to stay safe? Name one resentment, large or quiet. Then, instead of turning away, write what it protected in you. Was it your sense of dignity? Your longing for fairness? Your inner child who once had no voice and now refuses to go unheard? Let this reflection be an act of reclamation—not forgiving before you are ready, not bypassing pain, but honoring the truth that has not yet been seen. What do you need to feel to release this? What conversation, boundary, or ritual might help you shift from holding on to being free? This does not mean reconnection. Some ties are best left severed. It means re-centering yourself after something pulled you off course. When you choose to face resentment with gentle honesty, you stop carrying it as punishment. You begin holding it as wisdom. And from there, freedom is not only possible—it begins.

Think of the resilience that grew inside you in the space where resentment once settled. How can you thank yourself for surviving what you should never have had to carry— and for being brave enough now to face it with truth and care?

_____

_____

_____

_____

_____

_____

_____

_____

_____

_____

_____

_____

_____

_____

_____

_____

_____

_____

_____

_____

_____

_____

_____

_____

DAY 46

The weight is still mine—

not from what they did or said,

but from what I clutch.

Forgiveness is not a door you open for the one who hurt you—it is the key that frees your own hands. Often misunderstood as absolution or forgetting, true forgiveness is not about pretending harm never happened. It is about ending the cycle where you relive it, rehearse it, and carry it like armor you never wanted to wear. That armor may have once felt necessary—a shield against further pain—but over time, it becomes a weight that exhausts you, distorts your posture, and limits your reach. What might you recover in yourself if you put this weight down—not for them to feel better, but for you to breathe again? Write about the harm. Not to excuse it, but to see it clearly, as it was. What did you lose in that experience—trust, dignity, peace, and perhaps even a sense of belonging or safety in your own skin? And now, ask yourself: what have you continued to lose by keeping the pain alive through resentment, silence, or the quiet belief that healing is betrayal? The mind often tells us that forgiveness is weakness. But true forgiveness is radical—it requires deep clarity, fierce boundaries, and a willingness to stop dragging the wound forward. It is not passive. It is not naive. It is a conscious refusal to let someone else's cruelty or carelessness define your life. List one belief you have built from that harm—perhaps "I am not safe," or "People always leave." How has that belief shaped your choices, your relationships, your ability to receive joy without suspicion or apology? How many times have you turned away from something good because it didn't match the story pain taught you to expect? Now imagine who you might become if that belief were no longer governing your life. Imagine the space that would open up—in your chest, in your calendar, in your capacity to trust your own worth. Forgiveness becomes a way of reclaiming possibility. You do not need to offer a second chance. You do not need a conversation. You do not need their remorse. You only need the courage to say: I am no longer willing to keep hurting myself for what someone else did. Forgiveness does not rebuild the past. It restores your access to the future. It is not a gift to the offender. It is a homecoming to yourself.

In what ways has your willingness to consider forgiveness opened space inside you? How can you thank yourself for choosing freedom over fury—and for protecting your peace without needing someone else to make it right?

_____

_____

_____

_____

_____

_____

_____

_____

_____

_____

_____

_____

_____

_____

_____

_____

_____

_____

_____

DAY 47

The bridge split mid-step —

yet even in the falling,

I found firmer ground.

When a relationship ruptures, it rarely breaks clean. There are the echoes of things unsaid, the tangled timelines of blame, the ache of what could have been. The silence after the final word can feel louder than any argument. And yet, beneath that wreckage, something else can emerge—something raw, honest, and unfiltered: the truth of who you became in the aftermath. Pain has a way of revealing not only what was broken between you and the other, but what was long neglected within yourself. What did this rupture ask you to confront in yourself? What were you tolerating in the name of connection? Perhaps you abandoned your needs, or ignored early misalignments in the hope that love would eventually fill the gaps. Perhaps you gave more than you had, or stayed silent to avoid disapproval, mistaking peace for safety. These moments become mirrors. Not to shame you—but to return you to yourself. To show you the places where you shrank, bent, or blurred your edges in pursuit of closeness. Write one belief about yourself or others that this rupture helped clarify. Maybe it taught you to trust your instincts more quickly. Maybe it stripped away the illusion that love requires self-erasure. Or perhaps it revealed a deeper hunger—for truth, reciprocity, or emotional safety. Rather than asking why it fell apart, ask what it unearthed. What version of yourself are you now growing into because of this pain? Let that be the focus—not just the loss, but the shaping. Consider what boundaries you have built since, or what new ways of relating you have come to value. Maybe you've learned to speak more plainly. To ask for what you need without apology. To walk away when your nervous system says no, even if your heart still says maybe. Growth born of rupture is never easy, but it is often profound. It doesn't just change how you love—it changes how you live.

What strength, clarity, or wisdom did this relational rupture leave behind in you? How can you thank yourself for walking through it without turning to stone—and for honoring the pain not as the end of your story, but as part of your becoming?

_____

_____

_____

_____

_____

_____

_____

_____

_____

_____

_____

_____

_____

_____

_____

_____

_____

_____

_____

_____

_____

_____

DAY 48

It no longer fits—

the skin I once clung to tight

falls away in peace.

Change stirs within—not always loudly, but unmistakably, like the tide pulling you somewhere new. It doesn't always announce itself with clarity. Sometimes it arrives as restlessness, as discomfort in places that once felt like home. A version of yourself, once necessary for survival, begins to feel like a weight. A role you played, a belief you clung to, or a dynamic you stayed inside of—suddenly, it no longer belongs to who you are becoming. And so you begin the work of release. Not because the past was wrong, but because you are no longer willing to shape yourself around its limitations. Not because you regret who you were, but because you now recognize the cost of staying there. What were you finally ready to outgrow? Was it the need to prove your worth through perfection? The habit of dimming your light to make others more comfortable? The reflex to stay silent, to stay small, to stay safe? Write it down. Speak of it clearly, without shame. You wore it for a reason. It protected you, helped you belong, and gave you something to hold onto when the world felt uncertain. But now, that reason no longer holds you. Now, you are held by something else—something truer. Trace what that release made room for. Did it open space for your voice, your peace, your boundaries? Did it shift your relationships? Your dreams? Did it allow you to take up space without apology, or to rest without guilt? Allow yourself to grieve what you released, even if it was necessary—freedom is still a loss of familiarity. And still, you chose it. You chose yourself. Now, reflect on how you knew you were ready. Was it exhaustion? Was it a whisper inside that grew louder? Was it someone else's words—or the absence of their care—that finally drew the line? The signs are often subtle, but the turning point is real. Naming it is a way of honoring it. It's how you mark the moment you stopped abandoning yourself.

What courage did it take to let that part of your past go—and what did that release make possible in your life? How can you thank yourself for trusting the pull toward something truer, even before you knew exactly where it would lead?

_____

_____

_____

_____

_____

_____

_____

_____

_____

_____

_____

_____

_____

_____

_____

_____

_____

_____

_____

_____

_____

_____

_____

DAY 49

I built a shelter

from whatever I could find—

and it kept me safe.

Not all chapters are meant for growth—some are meant just to keep you alive, heartbeat by heartbeat. You made choices not because they were perfect, but because they were possible. You clung to silence, denial, overwork, withdrawal, or appeasement—not out of weakness, but out of instinct. You were doing the best you could with what you had and what you knew. And that is enough. And now, from the vantage point of healing, it can be tempting to look back and judge the version of you that coped with pain by whatever means were available. But pause here. Can you see that earlier self with less blame and more understanding? What did you not know yet? What tools had you not yet learned to hold? You did not have the language, the boundaries, the support, or the clarity that you hold now. But you still got yourself here. That version of you was resourceful. That version of you was brave. That version of you kept going when stopping felt like disappearing. Identify one coping behavior that once helped you endure, but now feels misaligned. Write about it—not to condemn it, but to honor its role in your becoming. Maybe it was overworking to feel worthy. Maybe it was people-pleasing to stay safe.

Maybe it was emotional numbing to avoid collapse. Who taught you that survival was something to be ashamed of? And are you willing to release that narrative in favor of one that includes grace? Consider writing a letter to your former self, not with corrections, but with compassion. Tell yourself what you now understand about their pain. Tell yourself you were not wrong for needing to get through. Tell yourself you are here now, holding what they could not carry forever. Forgiveness is not forgetting—it is remembering through the lens of care. When you forgive how you coped, you reconnect with the part of you that endured. That part is not broken—it is wise, creative, and deeply human.

What did your past coping strategies protect in you—and how can you thank that version of yourself for surviving long enough to bring you to this place of reflection, growth, and choice?

_____

_____

_____

_____

_____

_____

_____

_____

_____

_____

_____

_____

_____

_____

_____

_____

_____

_____

_____

Weekly Practice

Carve out one day to be alone this week—not as isolation, but as communion with your deeper self. Step away from the noise, the notifications, the constant pull of obligation. Walk a forest trail, sit by a body of water, or find a quiet corner of your home where silence can wrap around you. Let the stillness settle. Let it speak. Notice what thoughts rise in the absence of distraction. What parts of you speak only when the world is quiet? There may be discomfort—let it come, let it teach. There may also be insight, long buried beneath the rush of doing. Solitude is not an empty space; it is a sacred space. It is where the soul exhales.

It is where forgotten truths return with gentle insistence. Let this be a time of returning, of listening inward. You do not need to produce anything. You do not need to solve or fix or explain. Just be. Let your presence be enough. Let your breath be your anchor. Let your stillness be your sanctuary.

DAY 50

Alone is not lack—

I return to myself there,

not away from you.

There is a myth that needing space means something is wrong—with you, with the relationship, with your capacity to love. But solitude is not withdrawal. It is not absence. It is a returning, a recalibration. When you claim time alone, you are not abandoning others—you are anchoring yourself. You are choosing presence with your own soul, so that presence with others can be genuine, not strained. The deeper truth is this: when you deny your need for solitude, connection with others begins to feel performative, brittle, or heavy.

Reflect on the last time you felt overstretched in company—when presence began to feel like pressure. What signals did your body send? Fatigue? Irritability? Numbness? And did you listen? Or did shame override your need to step back? Write about the cost of pushing through. What did it take from you? What did it silence? Now imagine what it would look like to honor your need for solitude without apology? Create a ritual around it—not as retreat, but as restoration. Maybe it is a few hours unplugged, a walk without narration, or simply closing the door and letting silence speak. Begin communicating this need clearly, without cushioning it in guilt or excuses. Practice saying, "I need some space to come back to myself," and mean it as a form of care, not distance. You do not owe constant accessibility. You owe yourself the conditions in which you can hear your own thoughts, breathe at your own pace, and exist without translation. Solitude is not a flaw in your wiring—it is a part of your rhythm. The world may not reward it, but your inner world depends on it.

Let rise the memory of choosing your own company—and finding in it not emptiness, but restoration. What did that time restore within you—and how can you thank yourself for choosing space not as escape, but as an offering to your own wholeness?

_____

_____

_____

_____

_____

_____

_____

_____

_____

_____

_____

_____

_____

_____

_____

_____

_____

_____

_____

_____

_____

_____

_____

_____

DAY 51

One hand cups the flame—

ritual in quiet breath,

returning to now.

When the world moves unpredictably, gentle rituals can offer a kind of inner architecture—something sturdy beneath your shifting emotions. A quiet scaffolding. A rhythm that holds. Choose one daily gesture that you already perform—pouring water, brushing your hair, placing a hand over your heart—and slow it down, as if it is the only task that matters. Let your senses inhabit the act: the warmth, the rhythm, the scent, the sound. Invite yourself to move not for efficiency, but for connection. Let the motion become a meditation. A way of saying, I am here. Ask yourself: Where in my day does repetition bring a sense of steadiness? What gesture feels like it could become a doorway back to myself? There is no need to make it elaborate. What matters is that it is real—a felt rhythm, a place of return. With time, even the simplest motion can carry the weight of intention, becoming a reminder that presence does not need to be earned—it can be returned to, at will. Let your ritual whisper, "Peace is not far. It lives in the motion I choose to meet slowly."

What daily gesture has offered you a sense of calm or grounding recently? Give thanks for its presence—for how it held you, even briefly, when the world asked too much.

_____

_____

_____

_____

_____

_____

_____

_____

_____

_____

_____

_____

_____

_____

_____

_____

_____

_____

_____

_____

_____

_____

_____

_____

DAY 52

A thread in your hand—

not heavy, just remembering

what still holds you here.

Some objects carry a hush of comfort—not because they are grand, but because they remember what you forget in moments of overwhelm. A smooth stone warmed by your palm, a shawl that is wrapped around your shoulders through sorrow and stillness, the scent of a familiar tea steeping quietly beside you. These are more than things—they are companions, shaped by memory and infused with meaning. Notice which textures, scents, or sounds return you to your breath. Is there something nearby that feels like home to your nervous system? Something that softens the edges of your day? Choose one or two and place them within reach—not as decoration, but as offerings to your future self for when steadiness feels far. When unease hums in the background, reach for them with intention. Let them invite you back. Let them say, you are held. You do not have to hold yourself together without support. You never did. Sometimes the gentlest objects know the language of grounding better than words ever could. Sometimes, they speak in silence—and still, they are heard.

What familiar object, scent, or texture offered you a sense of safety or calm today? Offer your thanks—for the power it carries, and for your willingness to be soothed by something so tender.

_____

_____

_____

_____

_____

_____

_____

_____

_____

_____

_____

_____

_____

_____

_____

_____

_____

_____

_____

_____

_____

_____

_____

DAY 53

Safety, a whisper—

jaw unclenched, shoulders lowered,

feet remembering earth.

Safety does not always arrive with clarity—it often comes as a soft unfolding, sensed more than seen. A breath that deepens. A jaw that unclenches. A spine that lengthens without effort. Begin by listening inwardly: where does your body speak of safety? Is it in the way your breath slows around certain people, or the way your shoulder drops when you are alone in a familiar room? Trace these sensations gently, with no need for them to last. If the feeling feels distant, invite memory to guide you. Recall a moment when you felt at ease, understood, or at home in your own skin. What about that moment created space for your nervous system to settle? List three environments, relationships, or rhythms that support this feeling of steadiness. Then ask: how might I bring more of these into my day—not as escape, but as nourishment? Safety is not a reward for effort. It is not something you earn. It is a fundamental inner resource; naming it empowers your body to recognize it. To return to it. To trust it.

What reminded you that safety lives in your body, too? Offer thanks for that experience, and for your growing capacity to recognize and welcome it.

_____

_____

_____

_____

_____

_____

_____

_____

_____

_____

_____

_____

_____

_____

_____

_____

_____

_____

_____

_____

_____

_____

_____

_____

DAY 54

The crack in the wall

let in air, light, and the truth—

I'm still becoming.

Mistakes often echo louder than our intentions. They loop in the mind long after the moment has passed, rehearsed in harsher tones than anyone else might use. And yet, growth rarely occurs in perfection—it unfolds through the fumbling, through the missteps that reveal what we didn't yet know how to carry. What you call failure might have been your younger self reaching beyond their tools. Trying, stretching, hoping—without the skills yet to match the need. Today, write yourself a letter—not to erase what happened, but to hold it differently. Begin not with justification, but with tenderness. Speak to yourself the way you would to someone you love who is ashamed. Use your own name. Say what hurts. Say what you have learned. Say what you needed at that moment and did not yet have access to. What belief about yourself hardened after that mistake? Is it still true, or was it just born of the moment's heat? Let the letter hold contradiction—your responsibility *and* your humanity. Let it hold accountability and kindness. You are allowed to look at the damage without collapsing into it. You are allowed to repair without erasing the story. Place the letter somewhere sacred—your journal, a drawer, your pocket. Return to it when the shame resurfaces. Let it remind you that self-compassion is not earned by flawlessness, but it is earned by your willingness to remain in a relationship with yourself even when it is hard. Especially when it is hard.

Think of the mistake you have struggled to forgive. What new truth did it teach you, and how can you thank yourself for staying open enough to grow, even in the aftermath of falling?

_____

_____

_____

_____

_____

_____

_____

_____

_____

_____

_____

_____

_____

_____

_____

_____

_____

_____

_____

_____

_____

_____

_____

_____

DAY 55

The mask slips gently,

beneath it—raw, luminous,

a voice unafraid.

What if authenticity is not a fixed trait, but a current you step into—a living rhythm between who you are and who you allow to be seen? We often imagine authenticity as bold, loud, or unwavering. But more often, it's quiet. It is the soft decision to say no when you would rather please, or to choose truth over ease. It's refusing to betray yourself, even when silence would be simpler. Notice where your words feel tight in your chest, or where your 'yes' comes too fast—before you've checked in with yourself. Ask gently: What parts of yourself do you withhold in certain spaces? What do you shape to fit expectations, and what do you protect because it feels sacred? These questions aren't accusations—they're meant to reveal the quiet negotiations you make every day. The subtle ways you compromise, conceal, or contort yourself in pursuit of belonging. Authenticity isn't moral clarity. It's the embodied sense of being unmasked— rooted in your own truth, even when it's inconvenient, so ask: where do I bend too far, and where do I resist softening out of fear? Then, take inventory. Write a list of times you have felt aligned— when your words, choices, and presence felt congruent. Contrast them with moments you drifted—what pulled you away, and what called you back? This is not a performance. The goal is not to appear authentic, but to inhabit it. To let your decisions rise from that place, even when it is messy, even when it costs you approval. If you feel fragmented, start small. Choose one conversation where you will speak without distortion. You do not need to explain your wholeness. Just allow it to breathe. Let this be your practice: to return to yourself, to honor what is true, and to remain in relationship with your integrity—even when it's hard, especially when it's hard.

What is one space, relationship, or moment where you felt safe enough to be entirely yourself—and what are you most grateful for about that experience?

_____

_____

_____

_____

_____

_____

_____

_____

_____

_____

_____

_____

_____

_____

_____

_____

_____

_____

_____

_____

_____

_____

_____

_____

_____

_____

_____

_____

DAY 56

Roots press into earth,

not rushing the bloom to come—

still, the seed expands.

Growth asks not just for goals, but for care—an interior tending that often happens beneath the surface. Quietly, patiently, without applause. The version of you unfolding now does not need urgency or critique; it needs nourishment, space, and conscious attention. Begin with this question: What does your growing self long for most? It might be a rest after years of striving, or a challenge after too much shrinking. It might be softness, or structure, or simply the permission to pause. Listen without judgment. Let your answer rise slowly. Then, turn your attention to the patterns that shape your days: What habits sustain your clarity? Which ones scatter it? Consider the rituals, boundaries, and companions that help you grow in the direction you desire. Where do you override your needs to seem "together"? Where do you perform strength instead of practicing care? Let yourself name one way you have outgrown the version of yourself who once needed to survive differently. Honor that past self—but recognize that you no longer need all the same armor. Growth might ask you to revisit something you have put aside—joy, curiosity, desire. Or to leave behind a posture that once protected you but now prevents deeper connection. Write one way you will care for your emotional, spiritual, or physical well-being this week— not out of obligation, but devotion. What does nurturing look like when it is rooted in love, not self-improvement? Let this become a daily practice, even in the smallest decisions: the food you prepare, the conversations you allow, the way you speak to yourself. This path of becoming is not linear; it spirals, pauses, returns, and renews. And that is the beauty of it—you get to choose how you bloom.

What is one way you have already shown care to the version of you that is still unfolding—and how can you thank yourself for that devotion?

_____

_____

_____

_____

_____

_____

_____

_____

_____

_____

_____

_____

_____

_____

_____

_____

_____

_____

Weekly practice

Let your days be shaped by one quiet action—a gesture so small it might go unnoticed, yet powerful enough to mirror who you are becoming. If you want to be patient, pause and breathe when irritation arises. If you desire to be brave, speak the truth in one conversation, even if your voice shakes. These choices need not be loud or grand; they only need to be intentional. This is not a call to do more—it is an invitation to act meaningfully. To live with quiet purpose. At the end of each day, notice: Did I move in alignment with who I want to be? Not perfectly, but consciously. Let your choices begin to express your values—not someday, but now. You are not waiting to become—you are already becoming, in each quiet decision, each mindful breath, each brave word. Walk gently through your days, and let your actions reveal your soul—not through noise, but through presence.

DAY 57

A sudden sharp edge—

soft refuge calls quietly,

steadying the soul.

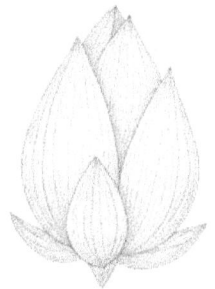

When the ground beneath your inner world shifts—whether from a harsh word, an unexpected change, or a memory that reverberates too loudly—resist the impulse to rush toward feeling "fine". That impulse to smooth things over quickly is understandable, but it often bypasses what your body truly needs. Instead, heed: What moves you from mere distraction into a genuine sense of protection? Understand that safety is not an instant switch but a field you return to patiently, over and over. Begin by crafting a space that holds you tenderly—perhaps lighting a candle, drawing the curtains, or wrapping yourself in fabric that soothes your skin. These gestures are not trivial—they are invitations to settle. Choose a phrase that grounds you and say it aloud with intention—something like "I give myself permission to slow," or "Each breath is a new beginning." Let the words land softly. Notice what brings a flicker of steadiness: is it the warmth against your skin? The gentle rhythm of your breath? The quiet hush of a room that feels like yours? These responses—warmth, stillness, and rhythm—are examples of the soft signals your body offers when it seeks refuge. Write down three such responses your body seems to welcome when the world feels too sharp; these become your personal map back to calm. Remember, rebuilding safety is not about reaching perfection, but about honoring yourself as someone worthy of care and protection.

What moments today offered you warmth, stillness, or steady rhythm? Hold gratitude for these gentle anchors and for your own willingness to meet yourself with compassion and care.

_____

_____

_____

_____

_____

_____

_____

_____

_____

_____

_____

_____

_____

_____

_____

_____

_____

_____

_____

_____

_____

_____

_____

DAY 58

Sacred lines drawn soft—

space blooms where respect begins,

the strength holds firm.

Your personal space, both seen and unseen, forms the foundation where your well-being takes root. It's shaped not just by what surrounds you, but by what you allow in, and what you choose to keep out. As you move through your days, begin to notice the subtle signals your body and mind send when boundaries are thinning—tension rising in your chest, a drain in your energy, or a restless mind seeking release. Rather than ignoring these cues, pause and listen. They are invitations to tend to yourself. Start small. Begin by naming one boundary that feels essential and manageable—perhaps a topic you wish to avoid, a task you cannot absorb, or the time you dedicate to others. Once you've named it, practice voicing this boundary with kindness, wrapped in quiet firmness, without the weight of over-explanation. Phrases like "I need some time for myself" or "I am not able to take that on right now" can become gentle declarations of your inner truth. After expressing your boundary, reflect on the moments when honoring these limitations brought you clarity or peace—how did your body soften, and how did your mind respond? Did your mind find space to breathe? These moments of clarity and peace are worth noticing. And if self-doubt or hesitation arises, consider how you might meet these feelings with gentle curiosity rather than harsh judgment. These feelings are part of the process—not signs of failure, but signals that you're growing. Remember, setting boundaries is not only an act of self-respect, but also a vital invitation for healthier, more authentic connections. Imagine how clearer limits might open pathways to deeper presence with yourself and others, nourishing your heart and mind. Each boundary drawn becomes a tender yes to your own needs and a firm foundation for your well-being to grow.

What strength can you find today to honor your limits? Give thanks for the moments when saying no became an act of care and created room for your peace and clarity to grow.

_____

_____

_____

_____

_____

_____

_____

_____

_____

_____

_____

_____

_____

_____

_____

_____

_____

_____

_____

_____

_____

_____

_____

DAY 59

Hands stretched every way—

still, someone will frown or leave.

You are not their cure.

Beneath the constant urge to please, grief often gathers—unseen but deeply felt. It lives in the quiet ways you contort yourself to be acceptable, agreeable, and wanted. At some point—perhaps early—you learned that peace could be kept by making yourself smaller, softer, more available. That being liked was safer than being honest. So you became the one who made things easier. You worked tirelessly, often invisibly, to carry the weight of everyone's comfort. Here's the truth: people's reactions are shaped by things far beyond you, but their fears, their histories, their unmet needs—these are not yours to hold. You are not responsible for all the ways others interpret your boundaries, your truth, or your silence. Pause and ask yourself: Where have you overridden your own voice just to keep someone from being upset? And what did it cost you? Write the names or memories of those you felt you failed to please. Now, beside each one, answer honestly: Were you abandoning yourself to stay in their favor? What part of you still believes that being agreeable equals being worthy? Begin the practice of release—not of caring less, but of no longer self-erasing to maintain harmony. Choose one space in your life where you will allow yourself to be fully honest, even if it risks disapproval. Practice saying, "This matters to me," or "I cannot do that," without layering it with apologies or justifications. Let discomfort come. It will pass. What remains is the strength of someone who has chosen truth over performance. You do not need to keep proving your goodness by sacrificing your wholeness. Some people will be disappointed. That is not a failure. That is a sign you are finally stepping out of the shape they needed you to be—and into the one that is real.

Call to mind when you upheld your boundaries, even when it cost you someone's approval. What part of you felt liberated in that choice—and how can you thank yourself for choosing alignment over approval?

_____

_____

_____

_____

_____

_____

_____

_____

_____

_____

_____

_____

_____

_____

_____

_____

_____

_____

_____

_____

_____

_____

_____

_____

DAY 60

Still, I say your name —

not to summon, but to hold

what absence once gave.

Longing is a form of love that has lost its anchor. It doesn't vanish when someone leaves, or when a chapter ends. It lingers in gestures you still reach for, in words you almost say, in routines that once held someone else's weight. It lives in the muscle memory of connection, even when that connection is gone. Missing someone, or something, is proof that it mattered, that it shaped you, even if it could not stay. Longing is not the absence of love; it is love with nowhere to land. Who or what do you miss right now? Name it without minimizing its place in your story. There is no need to justify your ache. Perhaps it is a person, long gone or recently distant. Perhaps it is a season of your life, a version of you that felt more alive, more certain, more held. Perhaps a dream that never came to be, or a place that once felt like home. Whatever it is, reflect on what it gave you, not just what you lost, but what was built within you because of it. What strength did it call forth? What tenderness did it awaken? Now ask: What longing have you buried because naming it feels too tender? What ache have you tucked away, believing that to speak it would make it too real, too heavy? We often silence our deepest longings not because they are unworthy, but because they feel too sacred to expose. Yet, what might shift if you made space for that ache, if you let it exist without erasing or explaining it? It is a sign that you remember. That you have loved, hoped, dreamed, and that those experiences left a mark. To miss something is to honor its impact. Let today be a moment to acknowledge your heartache without rushing to heal it. There is wisdom in simply letting it breathe. Longing is a compass pointing toward what makes you feel alive and whole. Let it guide you toward the life that still wants to be lived.

What did this person or season awaken in you that still lives on?

_____

_____

_____

_____

_____

_____

_____

_____

_____

_____

_____

_____

_____

_____

_____

_____

_____

_____

_____

_____

_____

_____

_____

_____

DAY 61

Beneath every name,

a pulse not tied to duty—

just breath, just being.

You are more than the labels stitched into your daily life—child, parent, partner, provider, achiever. These roles, though meaningful, are not the whole story. Beyond every checklist and calendar reminder, there lives a version of you untouched by performance. So pause. Breathe. Let your mind drift toward a quieter truth: Who were you before you were asked to be reliable? Before you shaped yourself around the expectations of others? It can be disorienting to peel back the layers. The roles we play often feel inseparable from who we are. But this reflection asks for courage—the kind that allows you to meet yourself in the in-between, where no one is watching and nothing is required. Sit with your name, and ask, what else lives here? What colors, desires, sensations, and memories belong to you alone—not inherited, not imposed? What parts of you have gone unnoticed, simply because they were never asked for? Consider the moments when you lost track of time, when the world dropped away, and you felt alive. What were you doing? Who were you with? Was anyone else even there? Now, think of one role that often defines you. If you gently set it down for a moment, who or what remains? Write freely from that place. Let your words surprise you. Let them wander, unmeasured and unjudged. The more fully you know the self beneath the roles, the more freely you can return to them—not as obligations, but as expressions of a centered, whole you.

What is one aspect of yourself that has nothing to do with being useful or needed—and how can you express gratitude for its calm, steady presence in your life?

_____

_____

_____

_____

_____

_____

_____

_____

_____

_____

_____

_____

_____

_____

_____

_____

_____

_____

_____

_____

_____

_____

_____

_____

_____

DAY 62

In me, worlds collide—

laughter woven through fault lines,

truth with trembling edge.

Your identity is not a single note—it is a layered composition, shaped by history, desire, resistance, and love. Some parts sing with ease. Others hold tension like a breath that never fully lands. So begin here: What facets of who you are feel like home, like return? What aspects have you felt you needed to hide, silence, or reshape to belong? Rather than seeking a resolution, let yourself witness the contradictions with no need to fix them. You may carry a heritage you love but also feel constrained by its weight. You may find joy in being a caregiver while simultaneously grieving the parts of yourself that get set aside. Which parts of your identity feel honored in your relationships and spaces—and which feel muted? Notice how you shift as you enter different rooms. What version of you walks in first? What version never gets to arrive? Create a list of roles, traits, and identities you claim or have been given. Write them down. Circle the ones that feel like gifts. Put a mark beside those that feel heavy. Do not judge—just observe. From there, choose one part that brings tension and write to it, not about it. Let it speak back. Let it tell you what it's been holding, what it longs for, what it knows. It may hold more truth than you've let yourself hear.

What is one aspect of who you are that brings you sincere joy—and how can you thank it today through care, expression, or permission to be more fully seen?

_____

_____

_____

_____

_____

_____

_____

_____

_____

_____

_____

_____

_____

_____

_____

_____

_____

_____

_____

_____

_____

_____

DAY 63

Molten at the core,

not yet shaped into a form —

but burning with will.

You are not fixed. You are not finished. You are a landscape in motion, a story mid-sentence, a flame learning its shape in the wind. The question is not what are you becoming, but how are you becoming yourself? We often search for answers in definitions — roles, titles, timelines. But becoming rarely follows a straight line. It curves, pauses, doubles back. It stumbles and sings. So instead of explanation, reach for an image. Let metaphor be your mirror. If your current becoming had a texture, a color, a rhythm—what would it be? Are you an ember, steady and slow, or a tidal wave crashing into something long overdue? Are you a cocoon unraveling thread by thread, or a river changing course through erosion and time? Let the image come without forcing it. Do not choose one that sounds poetic—find the one that feels honest. You might be scaffolding raw wood in the rain, unfinished but holding. You might be a bruise healing from the inside out, tender and true. You might be fog lifting slowly from a valley, revealing what's always been there. Or clay softening in warm hands, ready to be shaped but not rushed. Once you have found it, stay there. Let it speak. Write about what this metaphor teaches you about your process—your pace, your resistance, your courage. What do you need to continue becoming with integrity, not urgency? Let your image guide how you speak to yourself today. The molten core does not apologize for not yet being steel. The sapling does not need to be a tree to be whole. The tide does not ask permission to rise. And neither do you. You are becoming — not in spite of uncertainty, but because of it. Let that be enough.

What do you feel grateful for in your process of becoming—whether it is your resilience, your imagination, or the truth you are finally naming? Let that gratitude rise through you like warmth.

_____

_____

_____

_____

_____

_____

_____

_____

_____

_____

_____

_____

_____

_____

_____

_____

_____

_____

_____

_____

_____

_____

_____

_____

_____

Each dawn, the sun lays gold across the floor,
A silent gift we often just ignore.
Yet those who pause to whisper thanks at light
Will find their hearts less burdened than before.

Gratitude, a key of subtle grace,
Unlocks the joy time cannot erase.
It turns the simplest breath into a song—
A candle in the dark we all can face.

The world may shift, and fortunes rise and fall,
But thanks can steady us through it all.
For in the soul where thankfulness takes root,
Even sorrow feels a little small.

So drink not just from cups of gold and pride,
But sip the peace that thankful hearts confide.
For he who counts his blessings as they come
Will never walk with emptiness beside.

Weekly Practice

Select one self-care practice this week and tend to it as a ritual, not a task. This might be drinking more water and feeling how it blesses each cell, going to sleep earlier and noticing how dreams arrive more easily, or walking without headphones and hearing the sound of your footsteps. Whatever you choose, let this choice be a quiet act of devotion to your well-being. Not a checkbox. Not a performance. Just care, offered gently and without demand. Notice how your body responds—not to productivity, but to presence. To be met, not managed. Peace grows in well-tended soil. And you are that soil. This is not self-improvement. It is not a project. It is remembering you are already worthy of care—not because of what you do, but because of who you are. Let your care be gentle, consistent, and rooted in kindness. And if you forget, begin again. Rituals are not ruined by interruption—they are strengthened by return.

DAY 64

Whispers in the skin—

tiredness speaks before collapse,

listen while it is soft.

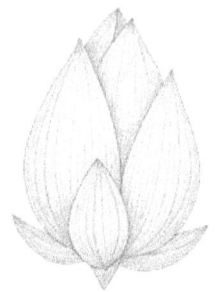

Before exhaustion becomes a shout, it often arrives as a murmur—a sharp sigh, a dropped focus, the quiet ache behind your eyes. These are not inconveniences. They are invitations. Attune to these early signals: when does your thinking blur, your patience thin, your limbs grow heavy? These moments are thresholds—subtle markers that you are nearing your edge. Rather than dismissing these cues as inconveniences, treat them as invitations to care. Create a simple guide for yourself—three signs your body gives when it is nearing its edge, and three gentle responses you can offer in return. Perhaps you stretch your spine with slow intention, step into fresh air for two minutes, or sip something warm without distraction. Maybe you close your eyes and let silence hold you for just a breath longer. Ask yourself: What have you sacrificed by pushing through these signals? And what might change if you honored them as sacred thresholds, not obstacles? Begin weaving subtle pauses into your day—not as interruptions, but as rituals that safeguard your presence. Let them be small, steady acts of devotion to your well-being. And let those around you know what support looks like when you are nearing depletion, so you do not carry it all alone. Rest is not what you do when you are finished; it's how you sustain what matters.

Think of one signal your body offered today—and how you responded with gentleness or care. Give thanks for your ability to listen inwardly, and for the choices that helped you feel more grounded and whole?

_____

_____

_____

_____

_____

_____

_____

_____

_____

_____

_____

_____

_____

_____

_____

_____

_____

_____

_____

_____

_____

_____

DAY 65

Night folds in softly—

your breath gathers the silence,

ready to let go.

The way you close your day carries you into the unseen hours. It shapes how you enter sleep, how you meet your dreams, how you begin again. Ask yourself: What helps your body know it is safe to rest? Begin with the senses. Explore the textures and tones that soothe—the softness of a blanket, the dim glow of a bedside lamp, the warmth of tea held between your palms, the hush of evening sounds that signal the world is winding down. Choose one comforting ritual and repeat it each night, not from habit, but as a way to say, *you may release this day*. It might be wrapping yourself in something familiar, placing a hand over your heart, or listening to a single song that slows your breath. Set a gentle boundary around bedtime—an hour when you ask the world to wait. Let this be your threshold, your invitation inward. As you prepare for sleep, whisper something kind to yourself: You have done enough. Notice what thoughts or tension arise as you shift toward stillness. You don't need to solve them. Just acknowledge them. Can you exhale them, even slightly? When you treat the end of your day as a return rather than a retreat, rest becomes an act of deep belonging. A way of coming home to yourself. And in that home, may you find softness. May you find peace. May you find the quiet truth that you are allowed to rest.

Bring to mind a part of your evening that brought you comfort—give thanks for its steadiness, and for your willingness to receive it.

_____

_____

_____

_____

_____

_____

_____

_____

_____

_____

_____

_____

_____

_____

_____

_____

_____

_____

_____

_____

_____

_____

_____

_____

_____

DAY 66

Years have slipped away,

yet the ache still knows my name—

I let it speak now.

Grief does not follow time. It follows meaning. A loss that occurred years ago can still stir something fresh in your chest, still rise at the sound of a song, the scent of a place, the turn of a season. It doesn't ask permission. It simply arrives. You may find yourself brushing it away with logic—*that was so long ago. You should be over this by now.* But the body does not operate on dismissal. It remembers. It holds what mattered. And tears are not regression—they are reverence. Let yourself feel what aspires to be felt, not because you are weak or stuck, but because you are human and the bond still matters. The world may have moved on, but your heart has not closed its door. So ask yourself gently: What loss still lives beneath the surface? Whose absence do you still carry, even if you do not speak their name aloud anymore? Write it down. Name what you lost, and name what it gave you. You may have built a whole life around the space that the absence left. That life is valid. Strong. Beautiful. And yet, the grief is still part of your architecture—woven into the walls, the windows, the way light enters your days. Allow yourself to cry if tears rise—not as a breakdown, but as a release. As a way of honoring that this person, this season, this dream once shaped your world. Consider creating a small ritual—not grand, but intentional. A candle lit in quiet remembrance. A letter written to what was. A walk where you carry their memory like a stone in your pocket. Let that ritual remind you that old grief is not an enemy—it is a thread in the tapestry of your becoming. To feel again is not to fall backward—it is to remember that your heart is still open—still capable of love, still shaped by connection, still alive.

Think of the one you grieve and ask yourself: What part of me did they help shape that I still carry with tenderness? How can you thank yourself for being brave enough to let that love move you, even now, even through tears?

_____

_____

_____

_____

_____

_____

_____

_____

_____

_____

_____

_____

_____

_____

_____

_____

_____

_____

_____

_____

_____

_____

_____

_____

_____

DAY 67

Grief is not a task—

it sits, breathes, unfolds, returns.

I walk beside it.

Grief does not follow a straight line. It does not move politely through five tidy stages or adhere to deadlines. It weaves, circles, disappears, then returns in full force—unexpected and uninvited. There may be days when you feel untouched by it, and others when the ache feels startlingly new again. That is not failure. That is fidelity. A sign that something mattered enough to leave an imprint that time alone cannot erase. Healing is not the end of grief. Sometimes, healing is simply learning how to live with the tenderness that remains. It's not about closure—it's about coexistence. About making space for sorrow without letting it consume you. About letting it walk beside you, not behind you. You do not need to fix your sorrow, nor do you need to justify its length. Where are you pressuring yourself to be further along than you are? Whose expectations are you trying to meet—your own, or someone else's comfort? Grief is not just about the moment of loss. It's about everything that came with it. The lost future. The unspoken goodbye. The version of yourself that was shaped in the aftermath. Write what your grief still wants to be seen for. Not just the event, but the layers underneath: the lost future, the unspoken goodbye, the versions of yourself that were shaped in the aftermath. Let the ache rise with no need to make it productive. Create space in your life that says, Grief is welcome here. Whether it is through writing, movement, prayer, or silence, there is room where your sorrow is not treated like a burden to solve, but a truth to honor. Some things deserve to be mourned again and again, not because you are broken, but because your heart is still in a relationship with what was lost. There is wisdom in not rushing what aches. And there is great love in allowing yourself to feel what still pulses beneath the surface. Let grief be a companion, not a condition. Let it remind you: you loved deeply. You still do.

Trace what your grief has carved into you—not just sorrow, but proof of how deeply you've lived and loved. How can you thank yourself for holding that tenderness without turning away—and for honoring your sorrow as something sacred, not inconvenient?

_____

_____

_____

_____

_____

_____

_____

_____

_____

_____

_____

_____

_____

_____

_____

_____

_____

_____

_____

_____

_____

_____

_____

DAY 68

Words untethered now —

drift across the silent space,

touching what remains.

Departure—whether through distance, time, or death—leaves behind unspoken words, unexpressed feelings, and questions that echo like incomplete songs, waiting for a final note that may never come. Writing to them—the ones who are gone—can be a way to hold those fragments, to give voice to what remains tangled inside your heart. To honor the bond that still pulses beneath the surface. Imagine the letter not as a conversation, but as a container for everything you long to say, without expectation of a reply. Who do you carry inside you still? What truths or forgiveness, love or regret, do you want to place gently on paper or in your mind? Allow yourself to speak freely—without censoring for fear or politeness. Without shaping your grief into something palatable. What did you never get to say? What do you wish they had known about you, about the relationship, about the space they left behind? Write as though they were sitting beside you. What stories would you tell? What apologies, thanks, or memories would you offer? If anger or sorrow arises, welcome it too. Healing is not about smoothing edges, but about allowing the full spectrum of feeling to be witnessed. Consider reading your letter aloud—into the air, into a journal, or even to an imagined listener. Notice what shifts inside you as the words move from within to the outside. Does it soften the ache? Does it bring clarity or stir new questions? This practice does not erase loss, but it reshapes your relationship with it. It becomes a bridge between what was and what still lives within you. A way to say: I remember. I still feel. I still care. And in that remembering, you honor not only them—but yourself. The one who loved. The one who lost. The one who continues.

Reflect on the courage it takes to hold these words and feelings and share them without expectation. How can you thank yourself for carrying both the pain and love?

_____

_____

_____

_____

_____

_____

_____

_____

_____

_____

_____

_____

_____

_____

_____

_____

_____

_____

_____

_____

_____

_____

_____

_____

DAY 69

Hands no longer clenched—

the wind still carries the seed,

though you did not plan.

Control can feel like safety, like a railing we grip to steady ourselves against the chaos of the unknown. It gives the illusion of order, of predictability, of being one step ahead. We cling to it in moments of doubt, believing that if we just hold on tightly enough, we can keep disappointment at bay, avoid loss, and prove our worth. Yet underneath the urge to control is often fear—of loss, disappointment, of not being enough. When you unclench, even just a little, something subtle shifts. You may first notice discomfort, then fatigue—the deep ache of effort spent trying to control what was never truly yours to command. You may feel exposed, vulnerable, as if stepping into a room without armor.

But stay with it. Beneath the ache is something else—something quieter, more spacious. A raw, unfamiliar freedom. It doesn't announce itself with fanfare. It arrives like a breeze through an open window, asking nothing, offering everything. It whispers: What if outcomes did not define your worth? What if you could offer your effort, your care, and your vision—with no need for the ending to look a certain way? Try tracing one area of your life where you have been gripping tightly. Maybe it's a relationship you're trying to preserve, a dream you're afraid to release, a version of yourself you're desperate to maintain. Ask yourself gently: What am I afraid would happen if I let go? What might become possible if I no longer needed it to unfold just so? Let yourself live these questions in real time. Not as a thought experiment, but as a practice. Let the dish be imperfect, the meeting be unfinished, the conversation be unresolved. Let yourself trust the wind a little. You might discover a spaciousness inside you, one that does not rely on guarantees, one that is not built on outcomes. A space where your presence is enough. Where your being is not a transaction, but a gift. Where life is not a performance, but a dance.

And in that dance, you may discover a rhythm that was waiting for you all along.

Can you name one thing you are grateful for that arrived without force, without being planned—something beautiful that surprised you when you released control? Let that memory remind you what is possible when you surrender the outcome.

_____

_____

_____

_____

_____

_____

_____

_____

_____

_____

_____

_____

_____

_____

_____

_____

_____

_____

DAY 70

The road bends again—

no map, only your own breath

to mark where you are.

Some seasons arrive without invitation. They don't knock, they don't ask—they simply enter, rearranging the furniture of your life. They shift the pace, reroute the course, and leave you grasping for certainty. In these times, it can feel unbearable not to know what is next. The mind scrambles for answers, for timelines, for a sense of control. But life does not always reward planning; it often honors presence instead. There is a kind of grace in surrendering to what is—not in resignation, but in recognition. When you release the pressure to arrive at some polished destination, you make space to notice what is unfolding now. The breath you hadn't realized you were holding. The small kindnesses. The subtle shifts. The way uncertainty, when met with openness, can become a teacher. What if this delay, this pause, this not-yet, was not punishment—but preparation? What if the waiting was not a void, but a womb? A place where something essential is being formed, quietly, beneath the surface. Reflect on a past turning point that seemed like a detour—but later revealed itself as necessary. Can you trace how it shaped your resilience or clarity? Often, you do not see the meaning until you have lived it. Now, gently turn inward. Try naming what is now unclear in your life. Where do you long for answers, yet find only silence? What might trust look like here—not trust in a perfect outcome, but faith in your ability to meet whatever comes? To adapt. To grow. To remain rooted even when the map disappears. Learning to trust the timing of your life is not passive; it is a commitment to stay open, engaged, and willing to grow—even without a timeline. Let the path remain misted. Let the questions remain unanswered. Keep walking anyway. Not because you know where you're going, but because you trust yourself to keep going—and that is enough.

Name one moment in your past when the delay or detour led to something profoundly meaningful. What are you grateful for now that came only because the path did not go as planned? Let this memory remind you that not knowing is not always a lack—it might be the doorway to something more.

_____

_____

_____

_____

_____

_____

_____

_____

_____

_____

_____

_____

_____

_____

_____

_____

_____

_____

_____

_____

_____

_____

Weekly Practice

Each day this week, speak your gratitude aloud. Not just in passing, not just in thought—but with intention. Let it be a practice, a ritual, a quiet rebellion against the rush of everyday life. Pause. Look into someone's eyes—your partner, barista, coworker, or child—and name something you appreciate about them. Be specific. "Thank you for your steadiness today," or "I noticed how carefully you listened." Let your words land like soft offerings. Watch how faces shift, shoulders ease. How something tender flickers in the space between you. Gratitude spoken aloud is a form of love made visible. You may find that the more you give it, the more attuned you become to the blessings surrounding you—not because life suddenly becomes perfect, but because your attention sharpens toward what is good. Let your voice become a channel for recognition. In doing so, you remind others—and yourself—what truly matters. That connection is sacred. That presence is powerful. That love, when named, grows. So begin. One moment, one sentence, one soul at a time. Speak what is true. Let it ripple outward.

Poppys

DAY 71

Silent whispers weigh,

skin holds storms and sacred light—

grace blooms in stillness.

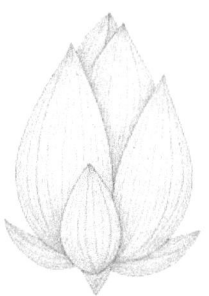

Begin by noticing the voice that lives beneath your mirror gaze—the one that assesses, pinches, hides. That voice may not be yours. It may be an echo of a culture that taught you that beauty means shrinking and that softness must be corrected. Ask: Who told me I had to change to be loved? What parts of me have I tried to make invisible? Let these questions settle like stones in water. You don't need immediate answers. Just the act of asking begins the unraveling. Now, replace these inherited scripts with gestures of reverence. As you brush your hair or step into the shower, whisper thanks to your body: for movement, for breath, for carrying grief and joy alike. As you touch the places you once shamed, imagine yourself writing a new story onto your skin—one where you are not a flaw to be hidden, but a witness to your own resilience. This is not about liking every part of yourself. It's about refusing to abandon the vessel that has never abandoned you. Each act of kindness—a gentle touch, a nourishing meal, a moment of rest—becomes a thread in the new story of your worth. A story stitched not with perfection, but with presence. Let this be your practice: To return to yourself, again and again, with tenderness. To honor the body not for how it looks, but for how it holds you. To speak to yourself as you would to someone you love.

What has your body done for you today that you can thank it for—not for how it looked, but for how it showed up?

_____

_____

_____

_____

_____

_____

_____

_____

_____

_____

_____

_____

_____

_____

_____

_____

_____

_____

_____

_____

_____

_____

_____

_____

_____

DAY 72

Warm sun on young skin,

Old laughter echoes—

Safety's gentle grace.

Journey back to the sunlit corners of your history, where a younger self knew only the profound ease of feeling secure. Let yourself linger there. Revisit a specific memory—a beloved space, a tender touch, a moment of pure, unburdened joy—and let its forgotten details resurface. Immerse yourself in the sensations of that past safety; feel the calm settling deep within your bones as if time has not passed. What specific circumstances, cherished presences, or unwavering truths provided the foundation for that deep security? Summon this feeling into your current breath, allowing its ancient comfort to infuse your present moments. Cultivate a conscious ritual where this innate sense of belonging becomes your steady anchor, reminding you that inner sanctuary is always within reach. Observe how this tender homecoming fortifies your spirit against the world's passing storms. How it softens your edges, steadies your breath, and restores your trust in the unfolding. This security—this deep, cellular knowing—is not a relic. It is a wellspring. And you can reawaken it, again and again.

With profound gratitude, recall a specific memory of feeling safe and loved in your youth. What enduring sense of inner peace or resilience are you thankful for that experience seeded within you?

_____

_____

_____

_____

_____

_____

_____

_____

_____

_____

_____

_____

_____

_____

_____

_____

_____

_____

_____

_____

_____

_____

_____

_____

DAY 73

The senses open—

threads of now, soft in your palm,

pull you back to peace.

When your mind scatters—drifting toward what has passed or what has yet to unfold—your body offers the way back. Choose one sense to explore, as if meeting it for the first time. Let your fingertips linger on the grain of a wooden table or trace the outline of a familiar object. Listen to the hum beneath silence, or notice how light spills across a surface near you. If one sense feels loud or too much, turn to another—your breath is not the only anchor. Your skin, your ears, your eyes—each offers a doorway back to now. Which sensation allows you to settle today? Notice the subtle shift when your awareness roots in the present—not just being here in body but also arriving emotionally. These practices are not about distraction; they are thresholds, openings into safety, clarity, and trust. With repetition, they become places of return—steady, faithful, and always nearby. In these sensory pauses, you remember that presence is not a destination, but something you can touch repeatedly. And in that touch—in that moment of noticing—you reclaim something essential. You remind yourself that you are here. That you are whole. That you are allowed to rest.

What moment of sensory presence today helped you feel more grounded or at ease? Offer thanks for the way your body brings you back to now—through texture, sound, or light.

_____

_____

_____

_____

_____

_____

_____

_____

_____

_____

_____

_____

_____

_____

_____

_____

_____

_____

_____

_____

_____

_____

_____

DAY 74

Bare feet on still earth—

a river moves through silence,

and so do you now.

When your thoughts scatter like leaves in the wind—restless, untethered, pulled toward past regrets or future unknowns—let the earth beneath you become a steady presence. It does not ask for an explanation. It simply waits, quiet and constant, offering its grounding without condition. Step outdoors—even for a few minutes. You don't need a forest or a mountaintop. A patch of grass, a tree-lined street, a balcony with sky above will do. And find one element of the natural world to witness with no need to shape the moment. Rest your hand on the bark of a tree, feel the weight of a stone, or trace the rhythm of a breeze across your skin. These are not distractions. They are invitations. Rather than asking nature to soothe you, notice how it exists—weathering, blooming, dissolving—without apology or rush. The tree does not hurry to grow. The cloud does not resist its drifting. The earth does not demand certainty. It teaches by being. Let your gaze meet the slow movement of a cloud or the intricate structure of a branch. What part of this stillness, this movement, echoes what you are feeling inside? Let that recognition be enough. If it helps, repeat a grounding phrase under your breath—"I belong," "I am steady," "This moment is whole." Over time, these moments will not live outside of you but will awaken within you—where the pace slows, the heart softens, and you remember your place in the world. This is how you return: not by force, but by noticing. Not by solving, but by being. And in that being, you find your way back to yourself.

What part of nature reflected something true in you today? Offer thanks—for the tree, the stone, the wind—for reminding you that steadiness and change can live together.

_____

_____

_____

_____

_____

_____

_____

_____

_____

_____

_____

_____

_____

_____

_____

_____

_____

_____

_____

_____

_____

_____

_____

DAY 75

A life leaves a trace—

not in noise, but in echoes

that nourish the soul.

Legacy is not always made of grand gestures or public recognition. Often it lives in the way someone felt heard in your presence, or in the tenderness you gave to something fragile. Your impact is not just what you do—it is what remains after you have left the room, the conversation, someone's life. What do you want to be remembered for—not just when you are gone, but tomorrow, next week, in the spaces you touch now? Is it the safety you create, the way you make people feel less alone, the truth you speak when it is hard? Trace the moments where your presence created change—not performance, but resonance. The quiet ripple of compassion. The steady hand in someone's storm. The way your words lingered long after you were gone. Legacy often reveals itself through longing. What do you long for more of in the world? Is it courage? Kindness? Clarity? That may be exactly where you are meant to contribute. Begin shaping your life to leave that behind—through your choices, your boundaries, your devotion. Look at your life like a landscape. What are you planting? What do you tend to? Where have you overgrown with effort in one direction, and what could you prune back to let more light through? You do not need a title or an audience to leave something lasting. You only need to live in alignment with what your heart knows is worthy. Let your legacy be a living thing—not a monument, but a garden. One that grows through presence, through intention, through love. And in that quiet tending, you become the kind of memory that softens others long after you're gone.

What are you grateful for in the way your life has already touched others—perhaps in ways you did not even realize at the time—and how might you let that awareness guide your next steps with intention?

_____

_____

_____

_____

_____

_____

_____

_____

_____

_____

_____

_____

_____

_____

_____

_____

_____

_____

_____

_____

_____

_____

DAY 76

A path with no map,

yet your feet still know the ground—

uncertainty breathes.

The belief that you must "have it all figured out" can become a tyrant, pressing against your joy, your spontaneity, your ability to begin. But life does not ask for mastery before motion. It asks for presence in the unknown and the courage to move before you understand exactly where the road leads. There may be seasons when clarity escapes you—not because you are failing, but because something new is still unfolding. Becoming is not a straight line. It is a spiral, a dance, a slow blooming. Allow the possibility that not knowing is a necessary part of becoming. Ask yourself where you are holding on tightly to control, and whether that grip is helping or exhausting you. Who taught you that your worth is measured in certainty? That confusion is shameful? Begin to question those inherited beliefs. They may have protected you once, but they may no longer serve the person you are becoming. Replace the pressure of having a five-year plan with the integrity of one honest step. Each decision does not have to be final. You can revise. You can change direction. You can choose something that fits the person you are becoming—not just the one you were told to be. Trust the process of self-clarity, not just the illusion of certainty. You do not owe the world a polished answer. You owe yourself the freedom to explore what feels meaningful now. Let this chapter of unknowing be spacious, curious, and infused with grace.

What part of your life once felt unclear, but eventually led you somewhere beautiful—and how can you honor that unfolding by being grateful for the wisdom that grows only through uncertainty?

_____

_____

_____

_____

_____

_____

_____

_____

_____

_____

_____

_____

_____

_____

_____

_____

_____

_____

_____

_____

_____

_____

_____

DAY 77

Wind through open doors—

each part of you fully here,

nothing pulled away.

Alignment is not a grand announcement. It often hums beneath the surface—a sense of integrity between your inner truth and outward choices. It's the feeling of being congruent, of not having to split yourself to belong. Recall a time when you felt yourself, when your words matched your beliefs, your actions felt meaningful, and your body was not bracing against itself. Maybe it was a conversation where you spoke freely, or a day when your energy flowed without resistance. What surrounded you then? Who were you with, and how did they respond to the most unguarded version of you? Ask yourself: what values were you living from? Were you prioritizing connection, rest, curiosity, expression, or something else entirely? What were you saying yes to—and what were you no longer tolerating? Write everything that was present at that moment—not only in your circumstances, but within your posture toward life. Did you trust yourself more? Did you listen without dismissal when your instincts spoke? Find out if anything from that time still feels reachable. Is there something you have since abandoned—not out of growth, but from forgetting your worth? From slipping into someone else's version of success or safety? Alignment does not always mean ease. It may ask you to make difficult choices, to walk away from what no longer fits, to protect truths that others may not understand. But it often brings clarity, steadiness, and a kind of internal exhale— the sense that you are no longer at war with yourself. You may reorient toward what makes you feel whole. Sometimes that means beginning again. Sometimes that means protecting a truth that once kept you steady. Let this be your invitation: to listen inward, to move with integrity, and to trust that the quiet hum of alignment is enough to guide you home.

What part of your past alignment are you most grateful for remembering today—and how might you honor that remembrance in the way you move forward now?

_____

_____

_____

_____

_____

_____

_____

_____

_____

_____

_____

_____

_____

_____

_____

_____

_____

_____

_____

_____

_____

_____

_____

Weekly practice

This week, follow a thread of curiosity wherever it wants to take you. Pick up a book that catches your eye, ask a question that has been lingering, try a recipe you have never tasted, or wander a path you have never walked. Do not seek a goal—let delight be the guide. Pay attention to what awakens wonder or surprise. Let go of needing to master or understand. Curiosity is not a means to an end—it's the soul's way of remembering aliveness. It is how we reconnect with the parts of ourselves that are playful, spontaneous, and free. By following it, you create space for joy and spontaneity to return. Let this be a week of unexpected discoveries, not answers. A week where you say yes to the unfamiliar, the whimsical, the quietly magical. A week where you remember that you are allowed to explore simply because it feels good. Because it reminds you that you are still growing, still wondering, still alive.

DAY 78

Crowded winds outside—

but beneath the noise, a hush

asks you to return.

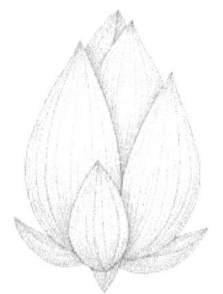

When the world swells with volume—demands, opinions, screens, schedules—it is difficult to distinguish what is sincerely yours. The noise is constant, persuasive. It pulls your attention outward, scattering your focus across a thousand expectations. The mind may echo with urgency, comparison, or chaos, yet beneath it all, a subtler rhythm waits. Listening inward is not an escape; it is a reclamation. It is choosing not to be pulled by every tide, but to anchor yourself in something deeper, quieter, more rooted. It is remembering that presence is not passive—it is powerful. Begin by noticing when your body tenses in response to external pressure. Where do you feel pulled too thin, overexposed, or scattered? Pause there. Instead of seeking another opinion or adding to the noise, ask yourself: What are you feeling beneath the swirl? What is mine to hold, and what is not? You might need to step away from a conversation, silence a notification, or set a firm boundary—not to shut out the world, but to tune back into your own frequency—the one that knows what matters, what feels true, what brings peace. This is an act of courage: to listen inward even when others expect answers, productivity, or agreement. You can build this muscle through practices that draw your attention inward—mindful walking, writing what feels unfiltered, or sitting with your hand on your chest until your breathing changes. These are not grand gestures. They are quiet revolutions. Let your inner voice be less about words and more about sensation and clarity. Over time, it grows clearer. And in that clarity, you begin to move differently—not in reaction, but in resonance.

Think of a time when you listened to your own knowing rather than the loudness around you—and it led to clarity, peace, or right action. What did you learn about yourself through that moment? Offer thanks for your inner compass, however faint or flickering it may feel. It is still there, always calling you home.

_____

_____

_____

_____

_____

_____

_____

_____

_____

_____

_____

_____

_____

_____

_____

_____

_____

_____

_____

_____

_____

_____

_____

DAY 79

Roots grow underground—

not seen, yet they know the path

toward light, still unseen.

Trusting life is not an abstract comfort but a muscle built through trembling, through staying when you want to flee, through listening even when the next step is unmarked. It is the decision to unclench your jaw when the answer has not arrived, to breathe into the ache of not knowing, and still say *yes* to the day ahead. It means recognizing that life is not a riddle to be solved, but a river you can learn to float in—even when the current feels unkind. It is learning to move with, rather than against, the unfolding. Where do you override your own intuition in favor of control? What part of you believes safety can only come through certainty? Let yourself recall a time when something unfolded without your interference—when life offered a path you could not have planned, yet it carried you exactly where you needed to be. Was that moment a fluke, or could it be evidence? Evidence that life, even in its unpredictability, has a way of holding you. Consider tracing how life has held you through detours, through losses that remade you, through doors you did not choose that led to truths you now would not trade.

Let today be a practice in leaning slightly less on force and slightly more on listening—to your body, to the season you are in, to the subtle cues you've learned to ignore.

You do not have to trust everything at once. Begin with something small: a conversation, a choice, a release. What if you did not interfere here? What might life know better than you do? Trust, in its most embodied form, is not the absence of fear. It is the willingness to walk beside it with no need for every sign in place. To believe, even in uncertainty, that you are not lost—you are simply in motion.

When life surprised you with care, ease, or beauty—without your planning or effort? Reflect on why you are grateful for that unfolding and how it might expand your capacity to trust today.

_____

_____

_____

_____

_____

_____

_____

_____

_____

_____

_____

_____

_____

_____

_____

_____

_____

_____

_____

_____

_____

_____

_____

DAY 80

Their eyes say, "I see,"

not as promise, but presence—

trust, steady as rain.

Think of someone in your life whose trust did not need to be declared—it was felt, lived, and extended in their steadiness and integrity. Perhaps they were not perfect, but they showed up when it mattered and never asked you to shrink to be worthy of their care. Their trust didn't mean certainty. It meant they let you be complex, let you falter, let you return. And in doing so, they offered something rare—a space where you didn't have to perform to belong. What did their way of trusting teach you about how to be with others? Did they listen with no need to fix you? Did they keep your story safe? Did they admit when they did not know, rather than pretending to lead? Now turn the mirror gentle toward yourself. How have you internalized—or resisted—that model? Where in your life do you extend trust conditionally, and where does hesitation come from — is it rooted in discernment, or in the fear of being hurt again? If you struggle to trust, begin with how it was modeled for you. Healing trust begins with awareness and continues with practice. What boundaries make trust sustainable for you? What invitations make it grow? Consider writing a letter to this person—not to send, but to name what they passed on to you through their being. They may have taught you that love is not earned through performance. Or that presence is worth more than perfection. Or that even in rupture, repair is possible. Let that learning move through you now, not as memory but as inheritance. Let it shape the way you show up for others. Let it soften the way you show up for yourself.

Trust, after all, is not a fixed state. It is a living practice. One that asks for courage, for patience, and for the willingness to begin again.

Who is one person—past or present—who showed you a kind of trust that allowed you to feel more fully yourself? What are you most grateful to them for, and how does their way of trusting continue to shape you today?

_____

_____

_____

_____

_____

_____

_____

_____

_____

_____

_____

_____

_____

_____

_____

_____

_____

_____

_____

_____

_____

_____

_____

DAY 81

Wounds stitched by your hands—

Not erased, but held with care.

This is how light lives.

Wholeness is not an achievement. It is a slow reunion—the quiet return of all that was once sent away. The forgotten, the feared, the misunderstood. It is the breath you catch after collapsing from the weight of pretending. The moment your shoulders drop and you stop performing for approval. To be whole is not to be polished, but to be honest with all that you are—including the contradictions, the longing, the shame, the raw aliveness. Consider the parts of you that you have tried to outrun—the ones that speak in trembling tones or arrive only in dreams. What if these, too, belong? What if they carry medicine you have not yet learned to receive? Wholeness asks you to turn toward them, not to fix, but to witness. You might begin by naming one trait, memory, or feeling you have disowned. Ask yourself how it shaped your becoming—how it protected, distorted, or deepened you. Then imagine how it might move differently in your life if held with compassion, instead of resistance. What would shift if you stopped pushing it away and began to listen? Wholeness may also live in your body—in how you rest without earning it, in how you say no without apology. What rhythms make you feel intact, rather than split or scattered? Where do you feel most stitched-together—not by certainty, but by self-trust? Let this be the work: to include what once felt too tender to touch. To gather the pieces you left behind and welcome them home. Not all at once, but slowly. Gently. Faithfully. Because wholeness is not a destination. It is a practice. A remembering. A return.

Name one part of yourself that you used to judge or hide—and give thanks for the way it shaped your survival or expanded your depth. How has that part helped you come closer to something true?

_____

_____

_____

_____

_____

_____

_____

_____

_____

_____

_____

_____

_____

_____

_____

_____

_____

_____

_____

_____

_____

_____

_____

DAY 82

Two winds crossed my chest—

one longing, one letting go.

Still, I stood and breathed.

There are seasons when your body becomes a crossroads—a living threshold between truths that seem to cancel each other out. You may feel love and resentment toward the same person. You may grieve what you chose while still knowing it was right. You may ache for what you left behind while building something beautiful in its place. This is not a failure of clarity—it is the mark of becoming more alive, more capable of holding complexity. Think back to a moment when two opposing truths lived within you—and instead of forcing a choice, you let both breathe. Perhaps you forgave without forgetting. Perhaps you stepped forward even as fear clung to your ribs. When you said yes with trembling hands. Let yourself return to that time. What did it teach you about your emotional range? About your ability to sit with the ache of not-knowing? In a world that demands neatness—resolutions, answers, and certainty—choosing to remain in tension without collapse is an act of integrity. It reveals a deeper kind of strength: not domination, but inclusion. Ask yourself now: where do you feel pulled in two directions? What might shift if you honored both with no need to resolve them? You can write a dialogue between the two truths. Give each voice a name, a tone, a reason. Let them speak—not to conquer, but to understand each other. Then ask what it would look like to move from a place that respects both. This is the work of wholeness. Not to choose one truth over another, but to become the kind of person who can hold them both—gently, wisely, without rushing the ending.

Think of one contradiction you have carried—one that stretched your heart, even as it confused your mind. What wisdom did that experience bring? Offer gratitude for your capacity to live in the tension without losing yourself.

_____

_____

_____

_____

_____

_____

_____

_____

_____

_____

_____

_____

_____

_____

_____

_____

_____

_____

_____

_____

_____

_____

_____

_____

DAY 83

Storm inside may rage,

Soft whispers guide breath to calm—

Peace finds a gentle hold.

When the world's demands tighten their grip—deadlines pressing, voices rising, screens blinking—let your inner sanctuary become your refuge. You do not need to earn this space. You only need to remember it exists. Notice the subtle tremors of unrest; explore the areas where tension lingers inside you, without judgment. The tightness in your jaw. The flutter in your chest. The heaviness behind your eyes. Engage your senses: press a cool cloth to your neck, inhale a cherished scent, or hum a muted tune until its vibration settles your core. Guide your breath to a rhythmic dance—a slow intake, a longer exhale—allowing each cycle to soften the edges of disquiet. Consider a gentle, repetitive motion, like tracing patterns on your palm or swaying, inviting your nervous system to unwind. These movements speak directly to the body's need for rhythm, for reassurance, for release. Offer gentle, reassuring words to the fragile parts of your being that feel overwhelmed. This conscious tending to your spirit in moments of strain is not indulgence—it is resilience. It is how you stay with yourself instead of shutting down. How you build trust with your own presence. How you remind your body and mind that refuge is not somewhere far away—it is within you, always.

Let this be your practice: to return, again and again, to the sanctuary that lives inside you. To meet yourself with tenderness. To choose softness in a world that often demands hardness. And in that choosing, you become your own safe place.

What self-soothing technique helped today, and what does your body want you to remember about it for next time?

_____

_____

_____

_____

_____

_____

_____

_____

_____

_____

_____

_____

_____

_____

_____

_____

_____

_____

_____

_____

_____

_____

_____

_____

DAY 84

The wind needs no task—

it moves because it was born.

So do you, dear one.

There is an ache that comes from living as though stillness must be justified. You may not speak it aloud, but it lives in how you delay rest, in how you negotiate with your own softness. It's in the tension you carry, the way you brace against ease, as if comfort must be earned. What if you no longer needed to prove your value through exhaustion? What if rest wasn't a reward but a birthright? Consider the ways you've bartered away your calm—chasing approval, avoiding judgment, clinging to some measure of being "enough." Who taught you that peace must be paid for? And who profits from your depletion? What does it cost you to keep proving?" Begin rewriting that story—not with declarations, but with your body—let your shoulders drop without explanation, let your breath deepen without earning it. Let rest find you not at the end, but right here in the middle. Schedule ten minutes of non-productive rest today. Not as a treat, not as a break—but as communion. A quiet honoring of your own sacredness. Let comfort be a practice, not a prize. Notice how the earth rests, how the moon waxes and wanes without apology. How nothing in nature rushes to earn its place. You are not behind. You may stop running.

What did it feel like to rest without earning it—and what did that reveal about what you truly deserve?

_____

_____

_____

_____

_____

_____

_____

_____

_____

_____

_____

_____

_____

_____

_____

_____

_____

_____

_____

_____

_____

_____

_____

_____

Weekly Practice

Set aside quiet time this week to write a letter—not to someone else, but to yourself. Imagine you are writing from the voice of your future self, someone who has walked gently but faithfully toward what matters most. This version of you lives one or five years ahead—steady, wise, and rooted in clarity. Speak from their perspective. What have you let go of? What burdens no longer belong to you? What have you embraced with devotion—not out of obligation, but because it nourishes your spirit? How do you move through the world now—how do you speak, rest, love, and begin the day? Let the words flow as though you are reminding yourself of truths you've already known. This is not a list of goals, but a reminder of who you are becoming—a letter written in the language of becoming, not striving. Read it aloud when you finish. Let it echo like a promise made in stillness. Let it feel like home.

DAY 85

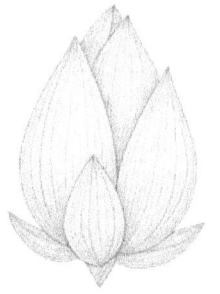

Once I wore their words,

stitched in silence to my skin—

now I grow my own.

Some stories are inherited before we even have language—passed down through glances, roles, the hush in a room when you entered too loudly. Others are built through repetition, spoken by others until you believed they were yours. "You are too much." "You are not enough." "You will never change." These stories cling, not because they are true, but because they were rehearsed. Worn into the fabric of your being like a familiar script. Yet there comes a time when a familiar story no longer fits—when repeating it begins to feel like betrayal. You may notice it first as irritation or a sense of shrinking in rooms that once felt safe. You may catch yourself in a script—people-pleasing, diminishing, doubting—and realize the words no longer belong to you. This is not shameful. This is growth. What narratives about yourself have become too tight, too brittle to carry forward? Write them out plainly—without sugarcoating, without judgment. Where did they come from? Who benefits when you believe them? Do they still feel alive, or are you keeping them alive out of habit? Now, imagine a truth rising beneath the rubble—a tender, defiant truth. One that sounds unfamiliar only because it has been silenced. Give it a voice. What does it know about you that your old stories could never name? Choose a symbol or phrase for this new self-story. Let it live somewhere visible—in your journal, on your wall, inside a poem. Practice speaking it aloud when the old ones try to return. Let it be your rehearsal for becoming. Because growth requires practice, too.

Reflect on a belief you once carried about yourself that no longer defines you. What helped you release it? Offer thanks for the resilience that allowed you to unlearn, and for the emerging truth that now seeks your care.

_____

_____

_____

_____

_____

_____

_____

_____

_____

_____

_____

_____

_____

_____

_____

_____

_____

_____

_____

_____

_____

_____

_____

_____

DAY 86

Hands full of old weight—

how can you climb with burden

you were not meant for?

There is a cost to carrying what no longer serves you. Even if it once protected you, even if it kept you tethered to something familiar—its weight now slows the rhythm of your becoming. What once felt like armor may now feel like a burden. What once tethered you to safety may now keep you from flight. Release is not abandonment. It is an act of discernment. And the first step in release is naming what has stayed too long. Is it a relationship where you bend yourself thin? A role you have outgrown but cling to out of duty or fear? A belief that whispers you are unworthy of joy unless you suffer for it first? Begin by writing what you are holding. Who would you be if you put this down? What part of you is afraid to? Release does not always arrive with a dramatic ending. Often it begins with saying no to the next yes that hurts you. In no longer explaining your softness as a flaw. In no longer returning to places that confuse your value with your usefulness. These are acts of courage. They are quiet revolutions. To honor this turning, create a ritual—however modest. Light a candle. Write a note and bury it beneath the soil. Speak the truth aloud in a room where you once stayed silent. Let your body feel the shift. Let your breath mark the moment. Stepping forward doesn't mean you know the next destination. It means you have chosen not to remain in a place where self-betrayal is the cost of belonging. It means you've decided that your becoming is worth more than your pretending. Let go—not to escape, but to make space. Space for the life that is asking to grow through you now. Space for the version of you that no longer needs to carry what was never hers to begin with.

Name something you will release—and give thanks for the role it once played in your life. Acknowledge the wisdom that allows you to part with what once felt essential. What new freedom does this make space for? Offer gratitude for the path ahead, even if its shape is not yet clear.

_____

_____

_____

_____

_____

_____

_____

_____

_____

_____

_____

_____

_____

_____

_____

_____

_____

_____

_____

_____

_____

_____

_____

DAY 87

No longer hiding—

this fire beneath your ribcage

was never too much.

Hiding, once protective, eventually becomes heavier than the courage it takes to be seen. At first, it may have felt like safety—a quiet shield against judgment, rejection, or misunderstanding. But over time, the cost of invisibility grows. You may have spent years shaping yourself into what others could accept—muting the brightness of your joy, trimming the edges of your brilliance, your insight, your depth. And yet, despite all the softening and shrinking, what lives inside you has never disappeared. Truth does not vanish in exile. It waits. Patiently. Faithfully. It waits for the moment you are ready to remember it. So ask yourself gently: What is one truth you have tucked away, not because it lacked value, but because it felt too raw, too loud, too wild, too holy? Is it your creativity that pulses just beneath the surface? Your fierce intuition that sees through the fog? Your longing for a different kind of life than the one you were taught to want? Begin by saying it aloud—just once. Let it echo in a space where you do not need to apologize for it. Let it ring true in your own ears before anyone else's. What relationships, roles, or inner contracts have required you to downplay this truth? What systems have rewarded your silence more than your authenticity? What would change if you no longer negotiated your worth for safety? You do not need a crowd to approve of your becoming. You need only your own honest "yes." A yes, that is unshaken by the absence of applause. A yes that honors your truth not as a liability, but as a sacred inheritance. Claiming the truth is not arrogance—it is reverence. It is acknowledging that you are not here to perform someone else's idea of who you should be. You are here to remember yourself. To return to the wholeness that was never truly lost, only hidden. Let this be a turning. Let this be the place where the truth becomes the foundation, not the burden. Where your voice is not trimmed to fit someone else's comfort. Where your life begins to reflect the depth you've always carried. You are not too much. You are not too late. You are simply ready.

What truth about yourself are you ready to no longer shrink from? Offer thanks for the way it has endured—even when unspoken. How has this truth tried to speak through you over the years? Thank the courage that rises in you now, the voice that is ready to be heard, and the path that opens when you walk with your whole self.

_____

_____

_____

_____

_____

_____

_____

_____

_____

_____

_____

_____

_____

_____

_____

_____

_____

_____

_____

_____

DAY 88

Grief carves open veins—

through loss, fierce roots find new strength,

love has quiet rebirth.

Grief is often seen as a shadow—something to outrun, suppress, or survive. But it is also a forge. It burns away illusion, reshapes identity, and transforms loss into a complex weave of endurance and tenderness. In its wake, we are not simply diminished—we are remade. When you examine the edges of your sorrow, you may find that grief has not only marked what has been taken—it has shaped how you now give and receive love. The pain, the absence, the longing—all deepen your capacity to hold both vulnerability and strength in the same breath. Grief teaches you to stretch, to soften, to endure. It teaches you that survival is not just about holding on—it's also about knowing when to let go. Reflect on moments when grief unexpectedly revealed resilience within you: the day you laughed again, not because the pain was gone, but because joy insisted on returning. Or when you set a boundary you once feared to draw, because loss taught you the value of your own peace. What did you learn about your capacity to survive, to hold on and release at once? Love after loss changes shape. It may become fiercer, more honest, or more cautious and deliberate, guarding the tender places grief has exposed. You may love with more urgency, unwilling to waste time on half-truths, or with gentleness, trusting that love need not be perfect to be real. Grief both fractures and builds. The tenderness it leaves behind can teach you to love differently—more openly, more truthfully. Perhaps it has sharpened your attention to presence—the way someone listens, the way they stay. Perhaps it has deepened your empathy, allowing you to hold space without needing to fix. Or it may have strengthened your resolve to protect your heart, offering it only where it is met with care. Let these lessons settle in your hands and your heart. Grief refines you—soft yet strong.

How will you honor what it's taught? What practice embodies your new way of loving?

_____

_____

_____

_____

_____

_____

_____

_____

_____

_____

_____

_____

_____

_____

_____

_____

_____

_____

_____

_____

_____

_____

_____

_____

DAY 89

Thread between fingers,

each loop pulling you back in—

a rhythm of peace.

Somewhere in the repetition, the body remembers what the mind forgets: how to stay. When life scatters your attention—when the days blur and the edges of your presence begin to fray—anchoring doesn't always come through thought. Sometimes, it arrives through motion. Quiet, steady motion that asks little of your intellect but much of your hands. Sweeping a floor. Stitching yarn. Folding laundry into crisp lines. Stirring a pot. Watering a plant. It is not the task that matters, but the tether it creates—drawing you out of the noise and into your breath. Let yourself lean into these rhythms, not as chores to be completed, but as rituals of reclamation. What movement helps you re-enter your body? Which daily motions calm your inner restlessness, even if no one sees them? Bring awareness into the motion: the pressure of your fingertips, the pull of the fabric, the warmth of your own skin moving through space. What do you feel when you slow into this rhythm without needing to perform it perfectly? What shifts in you when the goal is not productivity, but presence? You do not always need words to return to yourself. Sometimes it is enough to sweep the same corner again, to wind thread into form, to stir, to rock, to repeat. The body knows how to stay when the world feels like too much. Let it show you. Let your hands remind your heart that grounding is not found in stillness alone, but in steady presence. This is not about escape. It is about remembering that you are still here—alive, moving, whole.

What rhythmic motions have helped carry you through moments of overwhelm or disconnection? Offer thanks for the way your hands know how to guide you home when your thoughts scatter. Name one repeated action you have overlooked and let yourself feel gratitude for how it has steadied you—quietly, faithfully, again and again.

_____
_____
_____
_____
_____
_____
_____
_____
_____
_____
_____
_____
_____
_____
_____
_____
_____
_____
_____
_____
_____
_____
_____
_____
_____

DAY 90

Inside the silence,

a voice that does not tremble—

name made of strength.

When certainty dissolves, the mind scrambles for control—grasping for outcomes, searching for signs, bargaining with the unknown. It spins stories, forecasts futures, and clings to plans as if they could anchor the heart in a storm. But often what's needed in these moments is not more control, not more mental gymnastics, but a return to something quieter. Something older, something already within you. It is the part of you that has endured the unraveling before. Think back to a time you did not know how things would turn out. To the time when the job was slipping through your fingers. To the moment when someone you loved walked away. To the season when the next version of your life hadn't yet formed, and all you had was fog. Still, something rose in you. You chose not to disappear. That choice carried you. It was not dramatic, but it was powerful. Perhaps it was your deep listening, your steadfast presence in chaos, or your instinct to soften rather than harden that was key. This is an inner resource—not abstract, but alive. One you have already drawn on, one that carried you when the ground was unsteady. One that whispered when everything else was loud. Give it a name. Let it become part of your language of self-trust. Call it resilience. Call it grace. Call it your compass. Not hope as dreaming, but hope as a practiced muscle. Not patience as passivity, but patience as a sacred strategy. Write about this part of yourself in the present tense. It is with me now. It knows what to do. It does not need proof to act with wisdom. You are not without direction. You are not lost. The compass is already within you. Let it guide your next breath, not just your next plan.

What part of you has remained steady when fear filled the room—and can you feel gratitude for the way it shows up, even when no one else sees it?

_____

_____

_____

_____

_____

_____

_____

_____

_____

_____

_____

_____

_____

_____

_____

_____

_____

_____

_____

_____

_____

_____

_____

_____

Final Reflection: A Return to Self

This final page is not a farewell, but a gentle turning—like the last ember before dawn, still warm with meaning, still glowing with memory. You have wandered through tenderness and rupture, through silence and awakening. You have named shadows, honored longing, reclaimed forgotten truths. Page by page, you have gathered yourself, not in pursuit of perfection, but in devotion to presence. This journal has held your questions, your contradictions, your becoming. It has witnessed your unraveling and your reweaving. It has been a quiet companion to your inner work. And scattered through it all, like stars stitched into dusk, were moments of light. These moments—of honesty, of courage, of small self-forgivings—are the lamps we carry forward. They do not promise certainty, but they remind us: you are still here, and that matters. Now, let this chapter close with reverence. Pause and ask: What have you unearthed? What truths surprised you? Where did you break, and where did you mend? What kind of light have you come to trust in yourself?

Tuck this journal away like a letter to your future self. Return to it not as proof, but as a mirror. Let it reflect not just who you were, but who you are becoming. In a few years, open these pages again. Revisit the same questions. Trace what has softened, what has shifted, what has remained. Let your growth be marked not only by answers, but by how tenderly you hold the questions.

This journal is a constellation of your inner work. A map of your light, drawn one flicker at a time. A testament to your staying, your listening, your becoming.

May you never forget: Even in the unseen, the light within you remains.

You walked through storms with shadows at your side,
fell down, rose up, with no clear map to guide.
Yet every wound became a sacred sign—
each tear of a star the night could not deride.

You faced the mirror with a braver heart,
unlearned the lies that tore your truth apart.
And in the stillness, found what few embrace:
yourself—no longer breaking, but a work of art.

The hills you climbed were not in vain, but wise—
they taught your soul to see with deeper eyes.
And now, where once the ache of doubt would burn,
there blooms a peace that fear no more denies.

So take this moment, breathe, and gently bow—
you made it here, and who you are is how.
Through trials, love, and learning, you became
a light unto yourself—be proud, be now.

www.ingramcontent.com/pod-product-compliance
Lightning Source LLC
Chambersburg PA
CBHW081656120626
46550CB00010B/2919